This book was presented

to

Jackson State Community College

Library

by

Caring for the Parents Who Cared for You

CARING
for the
PARENTS
Who Cared for You

What to Do When an Aging Parent Needs You

Kenneth P. Scileppi, M.D.

A Birch Lane Press Book
Published by Carol Publishing Group

A Birch Lane Press Book
Published by Carol Publishing Group
Birch Lane Press is a registered trademark of Carol Communications, Inc.

Editorial, sales and distribution, rights and permissions inquiries should be addressed to Carol Publishing Group, 120 Enterprise Avenue, Secaucus, N.J. 07094

In Canada: Canadian Manda Group, One Atlantic Avenue, Suite 105, Toronto, Ontario, M6K 3E7

Carol Publishing Group books may be purchased in bulk at special discounts for sales promotion, fund-raising, or educational purposes. Special editions can be created to specifications. For details, contact Special Sales Department, 120 Enterprise Avenue, Secaucus, N.J. 07094.

Manufactured in the United States of America

10 9 8 7 6 5 4 3 2 1

Library of Congress Cataloging-in-Publication Data

Scileppi, Kenneth P.
    Caring for the parents who cared for you : what to do when an aging parent needs you / Kenneth P. Scileppi.
        p.   cm.
    "A Birch Lane Press book."
    ISBN 1-55972-367-X (hc)
    1. Aging parents—Care. 2. Aging parents—Family relationships.
3. Aging parents—Health and hygiene. 4. Adult children—Family relationships. I. Title.
HQ1063.6.S37   1996
306.874—dc20   96-28948
                                                     CIP

To my own parents and children with gratitude for all they have given me, and with hope that their places in my life never change.

Contents

Author to Reader

To open this book is to admit that you may be on the verge of undertaking a major transition in life. You must have realized that, before long, you may need to recast yourself not as your parent's child, but rather as your parent's parent.

To actually take control over the very same person who spawned and raised you as a child is one of life's most disquieting experiences. No one looks forward to such a prospect. For the average person, the idea of reversing roles with one's parent is so unpleasant that it is safe to guess that the title of this book would actually repel most browsers in a bookstore. Unless, of course, you have already been beset by doubts that *perhaps* something is seriously wrong with your mother or father. And unless, of course, you have realized that you are the only one who can do something about it.

When the circle of life turns, placing the care of a parent into the hands of a child, the comfortable, familiar patterns of family life must change. For the child, this always appears to be a shock. The prime virtue of family life has always been its stability and predictability—its inherent resistance to change. It is the family who always knows you as you really are; it is the family who can always see through transparent layers of acquired fame, position, and pose; it is the family who has always stood as a familiar and timeless haven into which one might slip when needing to recover from the bruises of the outside world, or merely to reorient one's psychological compass.

It is not surprising, then, that the prospect of rethinking and restructuring the roles of each member of the family is exceedingly unpleasant. It is an unwanted and uncomfortable process for everybody—both for the "losers" of familial power as well as for the "winners." Indeed, at times it is difficult to know whom to pity more.

Duty and circumstances, however, have always had a way of creating reluctant heroes out of ordinary human beings. Having a parent who is progressively failing may force you to acquire an unrehearsed set of skills—taking on the responsibility for the life of another adult. With the disappearance of the extended family over the past century, it is unlikely that you witnessed firsthand how to care for a parent whose health and faculties are failing. This book seeks in a small way to substitute for that experience.

Of course, learning caregiving skills by reading a manual is not really all that unfamiliar. After all, a manual on "adult care" simply mirrors the way in which many new parents read childcare books during the early years after the birth of their first baby. Many readers of this book have had their own upbringing influenced by such books as Dr. Spock's *Baby and Child Care*. Granted the dissimilarity in enthusiasm between caring for a newborn baby and caring for a failing parent, in terms of their essence the two actions are perfectly congruent. It is possible to study the one as well as the other.

However much information a book can provide, emotionally your transition into your parent's caregiver is certain to have its difficult moments. Regardless of how close and loving your relationship with your parents may have been up to this moment, the process of assuming responsibility for their welfare is not likely to be smooth. While babies fall naturally and comfortably under the authority of their parents, adult parents tend to resist with anger or depression any loss of control over their personal lives. It is not easy for an aging adult to know that the usurper of their autonomy is the very child they have raised!

Personal autonomy is seldom relinquished willingly. Determining the proper time to exercise your authority is difficult; so too is deciding how much independence your parent can safely handle. Despite your best intentions to be kind and sensitive, it is common for discussion of these emotionally charged issues to lead to twisted misperceptions. The results often are painfully hurt feelings—on all sides. No matter how "logical" or "unavoidable" it may appear that you should step in to help your failing mother or father, your parent may perceive your assistance only in terms of betrayal, greed, or conspiracy. These misperceptions, added to the natural difficulty of the task, can make an already un-welcome responsibility seem like a private hell.

And yet, keep in mind two important things as you take on this task. The first is that it is not a "private hell" that confronts you, but indeed a fairly public hell. Of the roughly 250 million Americans alive today, between six and seven million have some form of dementia. Since dementia is largely confined to the elderly population, this translates into an estimated 15 percent of Americans over the age of 65 having some degree of dementia. Even among the elderly, however, the statistics are skewed toward the very old being at greatest risk. Among the "youngest" of the elderly—the 65-year-olds—only 1 percent have dementia. From this 1 percent statistic, however, the prevalence of dementia doubles with every additional five years of age. By age 70 the risk is 2 percent. By 75 it is 4 percent, and so on, with the numbers multiplying in such a fashion that by age 85 one person in five suffers from dementia.

There are many, many adult children in your situation— enough to warrant a class designation as the "sandwich generation." With increasing longevity has come an histor-ically unparalleled situation. Large numbers of middle-aged adults are finding themselves—"sandwiched" between an unanticipated responsibility for the care of their parents and the unfinished task of helping their own children establish themselves as independent adults.

The fact that the problems you face have already been faced by others has made this book possible. The advice contained herein is based on the successes (and errors) of large numbers of middle-aged children struggling, on their own, to devise ways to help their failing parents through a series of difficult problems. After reading this book, you may be surprised to realize how much you know about the management of infirm adults. At times you may be shocked to discover how much more you know than the doctors on whom you might have blindly relied. Rather than rediscovering this expertise the hard way, by personal trial and error with your parent, you will be armed with very specific and detailed guidelines for each problem you are likely to face.

The second point to keep in mind is a prophetic one. Although you may not believe it at the present time, I shall state it anyway: Not until one year after your parent's death will you fully realize the magnitude and meaning of what you have accomplished. In that period of time your recollection of the innumerable daily problems and crises will fade away, leaving behind the memory of a unique and sacrificial act of love which you performed when no one else either could or would. The care of your parents, as they decline in their final years, will be revealed as the only act of love that might ever be comparable to the love and care which your parents once lavished on you. When you close this book for the last time, you will also close a circle of life and of love, so sweetly as to make you smile through the tears.

In reflection, you will be stunned to see the unexpected proof of your own emotional bravery. You will discover yourself to be much wiser and in possession of a maturity by then thoroughly seasoned. In your mind, you may hear the clear, pleased voice of your deceased parent, proud of how well you withstood the test and fulfilled all the hopes, dreams, and expectations they once conjured while watching you lie sleeping in your crib.

Consider again the title of this book. It presents itself as a guide to the care of failing elderly parents, and indeed this is true. Yet the hidden message of this book is that it is also a guide for you, a guide through a difficult rite of passage. You are about to take the last big step in growing up.

Caring for the Parents Who Cared for You

1

Why Parents Fail

THERE IS A DIFFERENCE between a sick parent and a failing one.

Your aged parent is probably very familiar with sickness, hopefully more familiar than you yourself will ever be. Today's elderly spent perhaps half of their lifetime in the pre-antibiotic era of medicine. Statistically, your parents were more likely to have been introduced personally to the issues of sickness and death at a far younger age than anyone in the generations that succeeded them. It would be surprising if your parents could not name at least one young brother, sister, cousin, or classmate who died in childhood of scarlet fever, whooping cough, diphtheria, or polio.

Your aged parent expects to be more prone to sickness with the passage of years, and recognizes the aches of arthritis, the visual failure cataracts, or the fatigue of a weak heart or lungs. In at least one sense, therefore, it is relatively easy to take care of a sick parent. You and your parent both see the problem for what it is, and can talk together about strategies to eliminate or cope with the problems of sickness.

But "failing" is very different. Failing means to be sick without the capacity to recognize what has gone wrong, or even that something is wrong. A "failing" mother or father is blind to the fact that with each passing day, he or she is less capable of living an independent adult life. It is like a cruel joke obvious to everyone except the victim. Because a failing older person will usually continue to feel perfectly capable, he or she may not be willing to listen to arguments that a problem exists. Feeling physically well, each day the failing parent drifts further and further from true wellness and, if not saved in time, is likely to suffer needless but irreparable harm.

"Dementia" is the word used by doctors and scientists to describe adults who once were perfectly normal people, both mentally and emotionally, but who at some point in their later years begin to gradually, progressively, and permanently lose their mental faculties. In the history of medical nomenclature, it is a relatively new term and replaces a host of terms now deemed "less correct"—in particular, "senility," "organic brain syndrome" (OBS) or "hardening of the arteries." Although the term is relatively new, older parents have been subject to the risk of "failing" for centuries. The problem has not changed much, despite having been recast in newer terminology.

In the technical language used by doctors and scientists, dementia is a syndrome, not a disease. There are a number of different diseases that actually underlie the state of dementia, but whatever the underlying cause—whether Alzheimer's disease or any of the other causes—the end results are remarkably similar. All dementing illnesses produce a progressive loss of memory, plus any combination of the following:

- depression
- difficulty in functioning in everyday life
- a change in personality and behavior

"Dementia" therefore is really a generic term. It is *not* a specific diagnosis by itself. Although it is true that statistically many demented persons have Alzheimer's disease, the term "dementia" is decidedly *not* just another name for Alzheimer's disease. There are at least a dozen different medical illnesses that can cause memory loss, mood changes, and a general dysfunction in daily living. Some of the diseases causing dementia are common and some are rare; more importantly, a few of the less common ones are curable, which Alzheimer's disease is not. Until you know exactly what kind of disease is present in your parent, the use of the word "dementia" represents at least an open-minded intellectual commitment to be mindful of things other than Alzheimer's disease when an older person has memory problems.

In the next few chapters, we will approach the problem of a failing parent in an orderly sequence of steps:

Step 1: Do you have good reason to be worried about your parent? Are the changes you're noticing about Mom or Dad truly the early changes of a dementing disease, or is it just normal aging viewed through your own anxieties? Chapter 2 explores some of the common characteristics of both aging and dementia, and offers some guidance about how to tell the difference. If you are fortunate, chapter 2 may be as far as you need to read.

Step 2: If a real possibility exists that your parent is starting to fail, what should you do? What diagnostic tests should be done? Chapter 3 reviews not only the common causes of dementia (Alzheimer's disease and small-stroke disease) but, more importantly, the uncommon *curable* causes of dementia, whose existence will go undiscovered unless someone thinks to test for them.

Step 3: Problem solving. Doctors may think that the diagnosis of a dementing illness like Alzheimer's is the end, but in fact it is only the beginning. Life goes on, even if it is a life marked by progressive failing over time. The "problem-solving" chapters of the book are roughly organized according to the progression of dementia, with the succeeding chapters tackling the problems of successively later stages of the disorder. These crude "stages" of dementia tend to reflect the extent of brain damage by the dementing illness. Ironically, life for you may be more difficult early in dementia, when your parent has failed only a little bit. In the early stages, there still remains a great deal of your parent's strength of personality, and you may have to deal with strong and forceful resistance to your efforts to provide some care or protection. Ironically, as dementia progresses and your parent's mental abilities continue to fail, so too will your parent's ability to argue with or mentally resist you.

It is easy to become overwhelmed and depressed as you read, chapter after chapter, of problem upon problem. Don't become too demoralized. No one failing parent is likely to have all of the problems considered in this book. Each person seems to present his or her own unique subset of difficulties. Which problems will actually surface in your own parent will vary according to prior personality tendencies, particularly their established lifelong habits of coping with stressful problems. Although some problems are universal—memory failure, for example—other aspects of dementia can be quite variable. Indeed, rarely I have seen dementia lead to a fairly tranquil state of indifference to worry.

You may encounter either a few or many of the situations and difficulties I discuss. Most importantly, it is unlikely you will run into any problems whose cause and treatment are not discussed in these pages.

— 2 —

Should I Worry?

SO FAR I HAVE BEEN deliberately imprecise about the signs of dementia. The reason for such imprecision is because the earliest signs are vague and difficult to pin down. People with different personalities, intellects, and educational levels will show such a variety of very early changes in personality, ambition, motivation, and intellectual expression as to nearly defy precise capture in words.

As a general rule, the earliest signs are almost never noticed by the parent and never mentioned by the family. Familial tolerance at the onset is understandable. Moments of memory failure are a universal experience, and it would appear inappropriate to raise such a dire possibility as dementia on the basis of a momentary lapse, a misspoken word, a still unfinished manuscript, an unmailed letter, or a wrong turn on an old familiar highway. Finding excuses is natural when everyone can identify with low-level random memory failures.

Yet the family's denial will usually go on much longer. It is truly amazing just how much dysfunction a loving family can overlook. The excuses, the explanations, the allowances—in short, the blindness of loving disbelief—will typically exist for two to five years before someone in the family finally voices the dreaded concern.

7

However long it takes, eventually *somebody* works up the courage to admit that there may be a problem with Mom or Dad. This is always a pivotal moment in the life of a family. Few issues appear so capable of sparking sibling conflict among adult children as the expression of doubt by one of them about a parent's mental capability. Although an emotionally healthy family may find that a parent's failing draws brothers and sisters instinctively into a mutual supportive alliance, other, less functional families may not fare so well. A discussion about Mom or Dad may quickly diverge back to unrelated arguments and accusations whose roots stretch back years and years.

Although the early signs of failing may be vague, by the time that the sons and daughters are openly discussing the issue it is usually due to the perception of problems in one of the following areas:

- memory problems
- social withdrawal
- financial errors

The following discussion may help register the appropriate degree of concern about Mom or Dad.

Memory Loss

All people become aware of problems with memory as they age, because some types of memory problems are a universal accompaniment of the aging process. Even in their thirties or forties, many slightly neurotic or hypochondriacal individuals accustomed to a superior memory may notice the memory changes of aging and panic that they are showing early signs of dementia!

All memory failure is not alike, however. There are two fundamentally different patterns of memory loss to recognize, and they carry two entirely different implications.

The normal memory loss that comes with aging has been called the "benign forgetfulness of aging." This kind of memory problem is a process that begins in the thirties and slowly worsens over the years. It is marked by a time delay in memory recall—that is to say, by an uncomfortable number of seconds before we finally remember what we're trying to remember.

As the decades go by, the number of seconds becomes larger. At age thirty, the pause may be only a few seconds. By mature old age, the lag time for recall may be measurable not in seconds but in minutes.

As a normal middle-aged adult, a few seconds' delay in memory recall may be only a minor inconvenience and easily disregarded. As the years go by, however, the time delay may grow sufficiently lengthy to cause noticeable frustration or actually handicap one's daily conversation. With sufficient recall delay, conversations become awkwardly and repeatedly interrupted, as names simply fail to come to mind in midsentence. Repeated verbal detours need to be found around missing words, making the speaker appear to others to be intellectually incapable of holding a normal conversation. Daily activities of living may become depressingly inefficient; for example, one may repeatedly forget why one originally came into the kitchen until one has left the room again.

Delay in recall is a handicap of an aging brain, but it is not dementia, and it does not mean that your parent is starting to fail. The hallmark of benign forgetfulness is that the thing to be remembered has not disappeared entirely from the person's memory file, nor does it entirely fail to pop into mind eventually. No matter how severe this memory recall difficulty may be, the normal elderly person will eventually remember. Such a person's speech and actions may have a superficial resemblance to the memory problems of a person with dementia, but it is only the time delay in memory recall that is tripping them up. Memory itself remains intact.

Difficulty with recall is not the memory loss that occurs with dementia. Not only is it not dementia, but neither does it evolve over time into dementia (although most of its victims are convinced that it will). This type of memory problem is an entirely separate process, and one of such universality as to be essentially a part of normal aging. If this type of memory difficulty is the sole issue afflicting your parent, then only patience, reassurance, and understanding will be needed—not medical tests.

It is the second type of forgetfulness, the so-called malignant variety of memory loss, that warrants concern and medical attention. In this case, little bits of remembered information which ought to be reasonably secure in one's memory seem to disappear.

The disturbing differences between the benign and the malignant forms of memory loss are perhaps most clearly illustrated in comparison. Typical examples of the differences involved might be the following:

Benign memory loss: difficulty for a minute remembering the name of someone's spouse at the family picnic a month ago

Malignant memory loss: mention of the family picnic last month evokes a blank stare or question—"What picnic?"

Benign memory loss: being angry with oneself for remembering Monday's doctor's appointment on Tuesday

Malignant memory loss: arguing with the appointment secretary that no appointment existed.

Malignant memory loss is the hallmark of dementia and one of the earliest certain signs of a failing parent. It constitutes a total loss of particular memories—memories that once were present and now have vanished. As a general rule, elderly persons who have malignant memory loss are largely unaware of it. They are less bothered about poor memory, perhaps in part because the very profundity of their loss leaves them unaware that something is missing. Truly demented persons complain very little themselves about their memory failure, unlike their healthy peers with benign forgetfulness, whose eventual recollection serves to constantly taunt them with repeated reminders of a memory problem.

Ironically, persons with malignant memory loss may

continue to appear fluid in their conversation, and their conversation may appear fairly normal so long as it is of the superficial social variety. Ironically, truly failing parents will often remain quite satisfied with themselves. Having genuinely less awareness of their lost memory, they tend to make fewer complaints about it. When they fail to recall a name or date, they are less likely to be frustrated or to find fault with themselves for being wrong. Often they continue to answer questions smoothly, even if incorrectly. Almost never do they correct themselves. If at some point they do admit to not knowing an answer, they often remain cheerful about it, excusing themselves that forgetfulness is natural for someone of their age, or explaining that they rarely pay attention to such things. They will improvise an explanation for stating the wrong date or day of the week by mentioning that they did not yet look at today's newspaper.

A tremendous amount of information can be obtained by identifying which pattern of memory loss your parent is showing. One simple test is to present your parent with a straightforward, pointed question that can be answered only via memory. How your parent responds to such a direct question in casual conversation speaks volumes about the presence of normal aging, dementia, or depression. For example, pose the question "What is today's date?"—either in casual conversation or point-blank—and observe the reaction.

Persons with benign memory loss are more susceptible to difficulty with their recall if suddenly put on the spot, so they naturally find difficulty with a direct question of this type. They will start to answer and then will probably hesitate—frustrated by a sudden unanticipated difficulty with memory retrieval. They tend to appear distressed at their failure, often because they too share your suspicions about their poor memory. By their body language, they reveal their torment, looking down or up or to the side, as if to find the lost memory that they know ought to be present. If you have the patience to wait, you may ultimately get your answer five or ten minutes later, as your parent announces today's date with whatever salvaged self-respect can be mustered after such a delay.

The classic response of the parent failing due to early dementia in this same situation is to avoid the question. This is not a deliberate attempt to cover their failure but is actually an accurate representation of the manner in which they disregard their own failing memory. Failing parents are genuinely and sincerely less aware of their poor memory. They honestly find little fault with themselves for not remembering and in general believe their own plentiful explanations for their failures. Because they "forget that they forget," each memory failure is their first and only. Your evident concern will appear overwrought, neurotic, and completely inappropriate. Asked point-blank "What is today's date?" therefore, the failing parent will either not bother to answer, offer an excuse, or try to slip jokingly out of the spotlight. "Who cares when you're retired?" You may see an effort to turn the tables, responding with a reassurance, dear, that nothing is wrong. Alternatively your parent may become indignant at such an impertinent question. Your failing parent may do or say anything—except answer the question correctly.

There is an important third response to the test question "What is today's date?" Persons with depression have some significant problems with their memories. Like the person afflicted with benign forgetfulness, depressed persons tend to be aware that they are functioning poorly, and are keenly self-critical. Similar to the demented person, they may appear unable to remember things on such a scale as to suggest malignant memory loss. However, some distinction between dementia, normality and depression can be made by examination of their answer to test questions.

Depressed persons tend to answer wrong initially but usually will self-correct not with the right answer, but with the explanation "I don't remember." Unlike the person with dementia, they appear to have awareness that they don't remember things. Depressed persons are different from the normal aged, however, in that they rarely spend time trying to answer the question. Rather, they will explain that they cannot remember things lately and let it go with that excuse.

The fact is, however, that the depressed person has not forgotten the date but exists in such a low state of mental energy that the effort of remembering is more of a burden than the effort of forgetting. A depressed parent will respond, "I don't remember," because it is the path of least resistance. If you, however, refuse to accept "I don't remember" and persist with the question three or four times more, you will probably get the correct answer. Typically it will be spoken in exasperation, as if to say, "There, you have what you want, now leave me alone."

General Rules of Memory Testing

- If your parent is complaining more often about poor memory than you are noticing memory lapses, the cause is probably normal aging.
- If your parent's memory is driving you crazy but is of no apparent concern to them, the possibility that your parent is starting to fail is very real. If your parent politely evades questions or unhesitatingly gives a wrong answer with no self-correction, you have reason to worry.
- If your parent accepts not being able to remember without a struggle and repeatedly responds to questions with "I don't know" rather than attempting an answer, be alert to the likely presence of depression.

How confident can you be in the results of this simple test? If the benign memory pattern is all that you are witnessing in your parent, you can stop worrying right now. Reassure your parent (and yourself) that all is well. If your parent's performance on memory questioning is suggestive of the pattern of malignant memory, then that *alone* is enough to warrant all of the diagnostic tests listed in the next chapter, even if for the time being no other problems are evident.

Social Withdrawal

At all ages of life, people seem to have an innate sense of how much social complexity they can handle. During the first two decades, as the young child's brain develops, there is a general expansion of confidence and curiosity. This expansion of one's intellectual horizons is made possible by the maturation of the brain. By middle age, a certain personal level of intellectual and emotional vitality has been established that is outwardly obvious and defines that person—whether sociable or solitary; a leader or follower; self-motivated or lazy; intellectually curious or disinterested. The broad horizons of a person's intellectual and social life are, by adulthood, fairly clear to one's family, friends, and coworkers.

Contrary to popular stereotypes, normal healthy aging does *not* change the person who we are. Talk with some healthy older people, and often they will confide that in their own minds they still feel very little different from when they were 18 years old, and they will tell you that they are often startled by the face that stares back at them in the mirror. With good health, personality remains intact with age. Despite the arbitrary rules of the Social Security system, *there is no evidence that any part of the human body or mind ages differently after crossing some magic age, including age 65.*

The aging process is one continuous, smooth affair that begins sometime in the late twenties. Throughout the passing decades, many biological aspects of our bodes may decline, but everything that changes from age alone does so smoothly, gradually, and without a sudden or sharp difference from one year to the next. Allowing for the formative effects of experience (both good and bad), the personality of an individual at age 50 or 60 ought to be easily recognizable at age 70 or 80.

The Social Withdrawal Rule: Any sudden change in the space of a year in your parent's social life, hobbies, or interests needs to be explained. If it cannot be explained in terms of sickness or environment, it should be considered a possible sign of failing due to dementia or depression. It should not be dismissed as simply "old age."

This rule specifies two important issues: the condition of your parent's physical health and the state of your parent's world.

Physical pain or the discomfort of chronic physical illness can restrict an elderly person's life without any dementing illness of the brain being present. Pain and body weakness are powerful incentives to remain at home, cut off from the world. Many medications, even at proper dosages, sap some degree of a person's physical strength and well-being. When physical sickness has caused visible physical impairments, a certain amount of negative change in a person's life habits may be easily explained. And at any age, there may be an element of pride and vanity for an ill person, two potent causes of social withdrawal.

As a marker for dementia, a second qualification of this rule on social withdrawal needs to be made. In examining a pattern of social withdrawl on the part of your parent, you need also to factor into your assessment any outside handicaps that may have been imposed involuntarily upon your parent. Retirement, for example, will usually force some degree of involuntary surrender of those intellectual and social activities related to the job. So too must one allow for the involuntary loss of your parent's personal network of friends, as contemporaries succumb to illness, death, or relocation. The key in this analysis is to honestly determine how much of your parent's reduced socialization is due to a loss of opportunity, how much due to a loss of physical ability, and how much is due to the loss of *desire*. It is in the loss of desire that dementia may be revealing itself.

You must examine carefully any signs in your parent of social or intellectual retreat. Despite their apparent banality, some common forms of everyday activity can be surprisingly revealing about the presence (or absence) of dementia, because doing these simple things requires an appreciable amount of "intellectual horsepower." Such "indicator" activities may serve as barometers of reassurance if they continue as part of your parent's daily routine. Likewise, if any of these indicator activities previously enjoyed by your parent should drop out of his or her repertoire, you ought to take serious notice:

- playing a game of bridge (or chess, etc.) to the satisfaction of one's partner (particularly if one can win)
- doing the Sunday *Times* crossword puzzle
- booking one's own vacation arrangements, with accommodations and travel
- dating
- reading a book from the current bestsellers list
- independently participating in a social organization

If the results of your parent's memory test were equivocal, it will be reassuring to note that any of the above is virtually incompatible with the presence of dementia.

Of course, not doing any of these things is of no significance if your parent *never* did them, but when someone who enjoyed the Sunday *Times* crossword puzzle for years has stopped doing it for the past year, an explanation needs to be found. It may be poor vision, or it may be early memory failure. The key here is to take note of significant sea changes in the social and intellectual life of your parent. A father who always cherished his good friends ought not to be finding excuses for not seeing his buddies. If the cause is not his arthritis, it may be that he is starting to find it too burdensome to remember all of the shared memories mentioned in their conversations. A mother who enjoyed playing cards ought not to be consistently missing games without some rationale that you yourself would find credible.

A curious thing about failing parents—it may not only be your parent who is appearing to withdraw socially from friends. Friends may no longer be showing up either. Close friends often begin to drift away when one of their party starts to fail, as if subconsciously sensing changes that are too frightening to acknowledge. If your parent's friends no longer come around, it should be considered an item of note.

Even before dementia affects old familiar social activities, it noticeably changes a person's capacity to adapt to new social situations. Dementia reduces a person's ability to cope with the complexity of change. As one's mental power weakens, the dynamic outside world begins to look threatening. A person's desire for the stimulation of new experiences simply evaporates when dementia begins to affect the brain.

In a transformation that is the reverse of the growth of brain power in the first two decades of life, a deteriorating brain finds pleasure in a few familiar faces and in a small familiar world. The idea of vacation travel no longer brings anticipated pleasure; instead, the idea of coping with new people and new places looms as a straining task better avoided. The effort and concentration it takes to deal with driving in traffic, parking the car, finding the theater, buying the tickets, finding one's seat—it all creates such exhaustion in the early demented person as to make the pursuit of recreation more tiring than refreshing. When parents begin to fail, invariably the greatest pleasure is to stay home.

Sadly, no discussion of social withdrawal would be complete without considering the most devastating of all losses— the loss of a spouse. This is a very special situation in the field of dementia. Very commonly, the presence of dementia in one parent will have been shielded from the rest of the family by the other parent, often for years. With the death of the protective parent, the full scope of confusion and dysfunction in the survivor becomes shockingly apparent to everyone. Only in retrospect is the extent of the cover-up revealed—the years of answers interjected by one parent to questions posed to the other, the word clues provided in conversation, the appearance of an ongoing social life.

Often in the wake of death, the children believe that this sudden change is emotional in nature, the temporary repercussion of the shock of death, which is too strong for their parent to bear. The children, who are also feeling grief, assume that they can extrapolate from their own grief and sense of loss to imagine how much worse it is for their mother or father, and hope that therein lies the reason for the dysfunction they witness.

Yet in the end, the same rules of life apply here as to the other losses of life. Natural grief for the death of a spouse is not an inherently different experience at one age or another. Recall that your mother or father may be more familiar with and seasoned by death than you are, having experienced a major world war and many having lost young siblings in the pre-antibiotic era. The allowances that can be made for grief ought not to be dramatically different for the surviving parent than for you, the surviving child. As with your own grief, there still ought to be evidence that whatever the shock, at the core your parent still remains functional.

Problems With Abstract Thought

Most people assume that the human brain is one organ, like the heart. This is not really true. We actually have—figuratively speaking—three brains dating to different periods of evolution and stacked one on top of the other. They even look different. Each has a different degree of sophistication, with Nature appearing to have devised more advanced versions of "brain" that it then grafted on top of the earlier models.

At the lowest level, we find our most primitive brain, sort of a swelled version of the spinal cord. At this most rudimentary level, the brain takes care of basic housekeeping functions that maintain life, like keeping the lungs breathing and the heart pumping.

More complex is the middle brain. Here we find a higher level of neurological sophistication that creates subconscious areas of complex movement. This brain can do amazingly difficult acts of coordination—walking, dancing, balancing, swallowing—all handled automatically and without intruding on consciousness. It can also feel emotions, and process decisions on the basis of reflex, instinct, and intuition. It can make associations between the senses and the emotions, reacting without having to "think" about it.

It is the third and highest level of brain that operates speech, language, and learned memory. These brain functions are handled by our most recently acquired, state-of-the-art brain, called the cerebral cortex. The cerebral cortex handles functions that are so complex that it takes about two decades of schooling to fully develop them. By the later teenage years, the cerebral cortex of the brain has sufficiently matured to tackle its most sophisticated task—abstract thinking.

Abstract thinking involves the use of symbols—a thing means not what the eye sees or the ear hears, but some other value that the brain assigns. Mathematics is a case of abstract thinking. It is not without reason that increasingly complex concepts related to numbers need to be gradually introduced, one year at a time, as children (and their brains) mature suffiently for each new level.

But there are other forms of abstract thought that are less evident than math. Proverbs, for example, rely for their wisdom upon the listener's ability for abstract thought and imaginative interpretation—taken literally, "A rolling stone gathers no moss" is nonsensical. Ideas of "distance" and "direction," as well as "time," are also abstractions. It is clear that certain levels of brain maturity are necessary to handle these concepts. Aggressively eager young parents who attempt to force-feed abstract thinking into their very young children find before long that the effort is pointless.

Dementia unravels the accomplishments of the human cortex, and does so in roughly the reverse order in which these accomplishments were achieved. The most recently developed abilities of the brain are the first to be lost, and that generally means the capability for abstract reasoning, whether verbal or mathematical. Problems arise in the subtraction of numbers earlier than in their addition, and there is a reduction in the sophistication of the person's vocubulary. Later may come the advancement of dementing illness into areas of memory, language, and mechanical skills.

Starting first with recent memories, dementia gradually

erases memory in a retrograde fashion, moving backward in time to erase ever more distant memories of a person's life. Simple sentences become impossible to complete, as more and more words disappear either from the vocabulary or fail to come to mind when needed. Fine motor skills begin to deteriorate. Ultimately dementia will progress into the deeper areas of our next level of brain, damaging automatic functions like walking and balance.

Your ability to discern whether your parent is suffering from early dementia depends upon whether you have some insight into how well he or she is handling abstract concepts. Making this judgment is sometimes easier in parents who achieved a very high order of intellectual accomplishment during their lives. College professors or authors who seem not quite able to focus on their next book or lecture; academics who have stopped publishing; musicians who no longer play new music—such changes may be the early signs of dementia or depression, but in either case are cause for concern. Ironically, for such intellectuals it may be almost impossible for doctors who do not know your parent to objectively diagnose a dementia-type memory loss by conventional tests at this stage. Having achieved an unusually high level of intellectual development in their lives such individuals may sustain a significant drop in their cognitive capacity that is clear to *you*, yet on standard testing may *still* fall within normal limits for the general population.

As with the investigation of memory, there are tests you can use to probe your parent's capability for abstract reasoning (if they will cooperate with you). One challenge is to serially subtract 7 from 100. Another is to ask your parent to explain several well-known proverbs, such as "A stitch in time saves nine" or "All that glitters is not gold." The answer should be correct. After all, they probably once taught you the meaning of these sayings. Fumbling literal answers point to a potential problem with early dementia.

For many parents, the earliest evidence of their intellectual decline in abstract thinking will be found in their inability to use simple arithmetic, particularly in personal finances. Those individuals who always did their own taxes may still do so, but the amount of time and anxiety spent preparing the papers and completing the return begins to increase astronomically. People who never needed a rigid written system to keep track of their finances now either forget to pay important utility bills or suddenly sprout notes on the refrigerator that say "Pay rent."

It is surprising how many adult children refuse to recognize the importance of this failure of arithmetic skill. Many children wrongly assume that to become confused by simple calculations is an accepted part of normal aging. Amazingly, many of these children may even have taken over the responsibility for their parent's financial affairs without consciously acknowledging that something about mom or dad is undeniably wrong.

Close attention to a parent's confidence and skill with mathematics is one of the most telling differentials between dementia and normality. A parent who can handle numbers well is probably fine. One who can move money from stocks to money markets appropriately, like the successful bridge player, can be left with peace of mind that there is no cause to worry about dementia. Still, it is not too drastic to advise that even one seriously delinquent utility bill or rent arrears warrants prompt concern and examination.

Conclusion

Memory loss, social withdrawal, loss of abstract intellectual function—these are the key ingredients of mental failing that will eventually force you to take some action to protect your parent. What does it mean if you recognize these changes in your own mother or father? If your parent has been showing these warning signs, medical evaluation is warranted. There is a 60 percent chance that dementia may in fact be present.

Sixty percent is a sobering number. Realize, however, that 60 percent is not 100 percent. It is vitally important at this point to make sure that you do not jump to conclusions. Before the words "dementia" or "Alzheimer's disease" are pronounced either by you or your family doctor, there must be absolute certainty regarding the following points:

- There must be a certainty that these troubling behaviors are not caused by psychological illness or depression. Depression can so cleverly imitate early Alzheimer's disease that no reputable geriatrician ever feels comfortable about making a diagnosis of dementia in a visibly sad patient. Unlike dementia, depression causes no brain damage and is completely reversible with the correct treatment. *It must not be overlooked!* Tragically, despite its "curability," depression can prove fatal either by suicide (sometimes motivated by a misjudgment that Alzheimer's disease is present) or by the health consequences of weight loss. The investigation of a possible depression should be made as outlined in chapter 3, until no reasonable doubt remains on the issue.
- There must be a certainty that your parent's behavioral or mental problems are not being caused by vitamin deficiency, toxins (including medications for other medical problems), or hormonal disturbance.
- There must be a certainty that the problem is not due to one of the less common, but more treatable, dementing illnesses that are not Alzheimer's disease.

If reading this chapter has given you reason to worry about possible dementia in your parent, the very next step is *not* to look up Alzheimer's disease in your home medical encyclopedia, but rather to set out on a search for all of those diseases that may be present and may mimic dementia.

As you read the next chapter, do so carefully and with some cautious optimism. Follow each step exactly, skipping none.

— 3 ——————————

What to Do First

IF SIGNS OF A DISTURBING CHANGE in memory, numerical dexterity, motivation, or overall socialization have appeared in your parent, it is important to act, and to act early.

Sadly, you yourself must shoulder a large part of the burden, ensuring that everything is done that ought to be done before a diagnosis of dementia is made in your father or mother. Too few doctors ever consider possible explanations beyond the ubiquitous diagnosis of "Alzheimer's disease." Perhaps it is because of the hypnotic effect of the mass media on doctors as much as on everyone else. Since the debut of the movie *On Golden Pond*, the media has unleashed a deluge of articles, TV shows, and movies about Alzheimer's disease. Fifteen years ago, Alzheimer's disease was a term that was seldom mentioned even in medical circles. Now everyone knows the term, and because of its too widespread popularity comes this warning:

If your parent is showing early signs of disturbing memory loss or behavioral changes, *you must not assume that it is Alzheimer's disease. If your doctor thinks he or she can simply examine your parent and make the diagnosis of Alzheimer's disease on the spot...find a new doctor!*

There are many steps that need to be taken in the diagnosis of dementia. It is not a simple matter, and there is no one single test that will suffice.

A growing number of interdisciplinary centers have sprung up around the country that focus on the diagnosis (and treatment) of dementia. Named for the most common type of dementia—Alzheimer's disease—these Alzheimer's Disease Centers bring together a variety of specialists— internists, neurologists, psychiatrists, and psychologists, as well as other related practitioners in physical therapy, occupational therapy, and social work. Throughout the country, there are twenty-eight major Alzheimer's Disease Centers funded by the National Institute of Aging, which not only provide an interdisciplinary diagnostic program but may also serve to allow selected persons access to experimental drugs not available to the general public. (See Appendix A.) The team approach attempts to provide the medical equivalent of one-stop shopping, not only for diagnosis but also for assistance and counseling to the family of the potential patient with dementia.

Compared to the average competency of a general physician in the community, these centers have several advantages:

- Potentially they offer a higher guarantee of quality as investigators.
- Some aspects of the exam (particularly the psychiatric portion) tend to be more acceptable to the patient if included as part of a package. Given the different cultural status of psychiatry earlier in this century, many of today's elderly still have negative feelings about psychiatrists. They will see a medical doctor willingly but deeply resent the suggestion that they consult a psychiatrist, which they believe means they are crazy.

Potential disadvantages of a multidisciplinary approach to the diagnostic exam also exist, however, including the following:

- The intensity of the exam can be overwhelming for an older person. By the end of the day, performances on some tests may appear worse than they really are due to fatigue. Even if the consultative service divides the examinations and tests into several days, the process can be exhausting for an older person to complete.

- There may be some element of intimidation in meeting so many strangers instead of starting with one known, familiar physician. Your parent may refuse to deal with the anxiety associated with such an evaluation but might be agreeable to seeing the family doctor.

Whether done by one's own physician in the community, or at a specialized diagnostic center, the medical part of the exam usually is performed first. Because of its more basic nature and because more of what the internist may find might ultimately be treatable, the medical examination occupies a key role. The physician performing this exam ought to be a board-certified internist, preferably one who also has additional board qualification in geriatric medicine.

Once the medical exam is completed, you should arrange an examination by a board-certified neurologist. This may be redundant if the internist is well qualified, but for an issue so important, it is good insurance to have the benefit of a second opinion from a neurologist. In particular, if over the past year or two your parent has shown any signs of the following, a neurological exam is essential:

- twitches, movement, or tremors of the hands or face
- falling or difficulty walking
- loss of control of urine
- periods of blank stares
- an epileptic-type seizure
- facial grimacing

So too if your parent's earlier life included an episode of head trauma, loss of consciousness, meningitis, or an occupational exposure to toxic metals, insecticides, or chemicals, a neurologist should be consulted.

The third appointment should be made with a psychiatrist. It is unlikely that the psychiatrist will render a firm opinion unless the preliminary medical and neurological investigations have been done first. The purpose of the psychiatric examination is to look closely for signs of depression. Depression is perhaps the *most* reversible cause of "dementia" that can be uncovered. The fact that it can so very nearly and superficially imitate a genuine dementing illness like Alzheimer's disease argues for a professionally guided search for its existence.

Strictly speaking, depression in not a true dementing illness. All dementing illnesses have in common the physical damage and destruction of brain tissue, although the means by which this is done varies from one dementing disease to the next. Depression may give the *appearance* of dementia but never causes actual brain damage of any type, and for this reason depression is often said to cause a "pseudodementia."

The pseudodementia of depression can fool even experienced doctors. As in a truly demented person, the individual with a depressive pseudodementia experiences difficulty with short-term memory, shows failings with job or task performance, and exhibits withdrawal from once enjoyable activities as well as social withdrawal. The effect of depression on the life of a human being captures nearly every worrisome sign discussed in chapter 2!

How can the one illness that does not actually damage the brain in any way nevertheless create such a close mimic of true dementia? The answer is that in depression, the problem is not that areas of the brain are being injured or damaged, but rather that areas of brain *function* are hampered because the subconscious is entirely preoccupied by the state of depression. Memory, for example, appears to be seriously deranged, but this is an illusion created by two features of depression—preoccupation and mental fatigue.

Depressed people whose subconscious minds are preoccupied with depression twenty-four hours a day are usually just going through the motions of daily living. They may believe they are capable of maintaining a normally functioning outer self despite their inner feelings, but this split between the outer and inner self causes havoc. They may be paying bills but mentally not fully paying attention to what they are doing. Numbers added up incorrectly go unnoticed; bills and letters mailed are returned without a stamp while others intended for the mail lie forgotten in a coat pocket. The scope of apparent memory dysfunction can appear to be so great as to resemble even severe dementia. The real dysfunction, however, is not memory loss but memory inattention due to a preoccupied mind.

The second mechanism by which a depressed person may display the appearance of dementia is due to the mental, psychological, and emotional fatigue that accompanies the depressed state. In a state of depression, it is a crushing burden to maintain social interaction with other people, a drain of limited mental energy to talk. Rather than create pleasure, socialization with others seems only to more acutely heighten one's own sense of detachment from the rest of the world. Depressed persons tend to be as economical with their conversation as possible and are quick with responses like "I forget" or "I don't remember," because such answers limit the effort expended in talking. As previously noted, if pestered repeatedly with the same question, however, not uncommonly the depressed person will suddenly "remember" the answer—the pseudo memory loss disappears when it becomes less of an effort to answer the question than to suffer the strain of repeated questioning.

The existence of depression in the elderly is sometimes overlooked because it is assumed, by general experience and logic, that a depressed person will always appear sad. In fact, persons with depression usually do appear sad, but not always. Sometimes an outward persona of cheerfulness may be maintained despite a seriously low mood. Not everyone will allow themselves the indulgence of public sadness or tears. This is especially true of the kind of person whose role in life has always been that of the "giver" rather than the "taker" in a family.

The psychiatric nickname for this phenomenon is "smiling depression." It tends to be most common in strong, confident persons, who within a family form natural anchors around which other family members tend to arrange themselves. Not infrequently this person is the mother or father of the clan. Afflicted with a depressive disorder, they are still making a conscious effort to appear "normal" consistent with their lifelong image. Whatever the emotional drain, they strive to remain cheerful in company, lest they burden their family with their emotional troubles.

Whether your parent is sad in appearance or not, therefore, an appointment with the psychiatrist is strongly advised if you have detected worrisome signs of social withdrawal or memory dysfunction. If any one of the following is true, it is mandatory:

- if your parent does maintain an outward appearance of sadness, even if this is only *your* opinion and not shared by the doctor
- if major memory difficulties at one moment seem to recede in the face of persistent questioning
- if there has been a loss of appetite
- if you witness or hear of unprovoked crying spells
- if there is a whispered story in the family about your parent's old "nervous breakdown" earlier in life, or if an aunt or uncle had a diagnosis of depression (depression has a tendency to cluster in families)
- if posing a direct question to your parent—"Are you depressed?"—evokes momentary hesitation, eyes filled with tears, or a simple "yes." I utilize this technique with great effectiveness, sometimes to the shock of family members who find such direct interrogation uncomfortably blunt. It is a trick especially effective with "smiling depression," particularly if administered with good eye contact and a soothing voice and delivered in an unexpected moment. Such a combination of tactics can shatter most façades
- and finally, if there is any doubt, for any reason, on the part of anyone in the family

In the course of these clinical exams, it is likely that a variety of laboratory tests have been ordered by the doctors. Take note of these laboratory tests, which should include the following (ask for a copy of all tests):

Complete Blood Count (CBC): This should be normal in all cases and preferably should be done outside of the doctor's office, by a large commercial laboratory (MetPath/Corning, Roche, Smith-Kline). Pay particular attention to the hemoglobin level. On most automated CBC machines, this is one of the prime measurements made and the most reliable in determining if an anemia (low red blood cell count) is present. Most doctors are fairly attentive to all of the numbers on this CBC test and focus in on any abnormality.

Perplexingly, however, some doctors have a confused idea that "a little anemia" is normal in old person, and erroneously allow more leeway in the hemoglobin level than they should. Sometimes old people do in fact have a mild anemia with no cause being found and no apparent ill effect, but it should not be assumed that a slight anemia is irrelevant unless further follow-up tests have been done and are all normal. If the hemoglobin is less than twelve grams per deciliter, ask the doctor if any workup has been done or is going to be done. If the response does not sit well with you, see another physician or a hematologist.

Complete SMA-20 Blood Chemistry Profile: These blood chemistry profiles are fairly standard nationwide now and are done with a high degree of reliability. Again, this should be done by a major outside lab (not the doctor's office staff). Many of the tests included in such a profile are not directly relevant to the kinds of disease that cause dementia, but some things are particularly relevant:

• Any abnormality of the *calcium* level should prompt a further check of parathyroid hormone; abnormally high or low calcium levels can cause mental dysfunction.

- Deviations of serum *sodium* can creep up on an elderly person and lead to confusion; if the sodium level is below 130, it is a possible culprit; if below 120, it is certainly at least part of the problem.
- Elevation of the blood *glucose* over 200 is cause for concern. This can mean diabetes, but of special importance in the elderly is the chronic state of dehydration seen in older persons with undiagnosed diabetes that can lead to weakness, dizziness, impaired concentration and disordered thinking. Additionally, if the blood sugar appears "good," but your parent is known to be a diabetic taking either pills or insulin, do not assume that everything is well. Some diabetics whose sugars are strictly controlled develop silent periods of low blood sugar (hypoglycemia) which over time can cause mental damage. If your diabetic parent is having "spells," this is important to investigate, but sometimes the hypoglycemia happens unwitnessed during sleep. If your parent is diabetic, and particularly if they report nightmares, have your doctor check the Hemoglobin A1C or Glycohemoglobin as well (these are specially requested tests) to gauge the likelihood of hypoglycemia.
- Abnormalities of the *liver functions* serum transaminase (SGOT or SGPT) may point to chronic liver disease. Liver disease does not only affect longtime drinkers of alcohol. Many cases of cirrhosis develop silently due to undiagnosed chronic hepatitis. If these routine tests show even slight elevations of liver functions, ask for a blood ammonia level. Also enquire if the doctor would send off special tests for copper and iron, since these elements play a part in some rare hereditary liver disorders that may have led to the nonalcoholic damage of your parent's liver.

Thyroid Function Tests: Sometimes these are done as part of the chemistry profile; sometimes they need to be ordered separately. Either way, you should ask for thyroid function tests (known to doctors informally by the shorthand

TFTs) and a TSH level. The TSH is an additional test of thyroid function that adds an important dimension of accuracy. Thyroid diseases are among the most prevalent diseases to imitate dementia in an older person, and the most curable if recognized. Make sure this test is done!

Vitamin B₁₂ and Folate Levels: These two vitamins are necessary for the health of all nerve tissue in the body, including the brain. Folate deficiency usually develops as a result of a diet poor in fresh fruit and vegetables. B_{12} deficiency, however, can develop even with a good diet—in fact, even if a supplemental B vitamin is taken! This happens because the vitamin B_{12} that is taken by mouth can be absorbed into the body only if the stomach makes a certain protein and releases it into the digestive tract. This protein is needed to pick up the vitamin B_{12} in the gut and bring it into the bloodstream. A significant number of older persons lose the ability to make this protein, and for them much or all of the vitamin B_{12} they consume may pass worthlessly out of their bodies. A vitamin B_{12} blood level test is an important test that must be done. For this test especially, check the computer printout to make sure that the specimen was prepared properly—unlike the other blood tests discussed here, the specimen for B_{12} needs to be frozen when it is sent to the lab (if it is carelessly allowed to arrive in a thawed state, the results may be worthless).

VDRL: This is a blood test for syphilis. Don't debate the issue—just get the test. It is a classic treatable cause of dementia, but understand two things: first, advanced syphilis is exceedingly rare nowadays; and second, some elderly people acquire a false positive to the standard test as they get older. A "false positive" in a laboratory test means that because of some technical problem, the test incorrectly comes out as if the person had the condition being screened for. In many elderly persons, a normal protein is present in their blood due to age, and this protein falsely triggers a mild positive reaction. Because syphilis is so rare, the odds of a false positive result in an older person are actually greater than the chance of a truly positive result. If the test comes back "positive," therefore, don't jump to any conclusions, either optimistic or shocking! Follow-up tests can be ordered by the doctor, and these should resolve the issue.

Heavy Metal Blood Levels: This standard test looks for high blood levels of three elements which are neurotoxic and can cause dementia—mercury, lead, and arsenic. If your parent worked in a factory (especially during World War II, when women did a great deal of home-front industrial work), this may be an important avenue to pursue. In cases of more recent toxic exposure, the source usually turns out to be some unsuspecting cause in the home, such as the use of unglazed pottery to hold citric juices (lead); flaking old paint (lead); old tooth fillings (mercury); or insecticide (arsenic). You need only do the test to have some assurance.

Electrocardiogram (EKG):   With this test, you are looking specifically for signs of excessive slowing of the heartbeat. Aging of the heart frequently affects the heart's natural pacemaker, causing it to erratically speed up or slow down. Sometimes the heart rate may go as slow as a rate of thirty to forty beats per minute. Many elderly persons at this slow rate will simply faint; others, however, can survive the sudden downshift in heart rate and keep standing, but the flow of blood to the brain is reduced enough to make them appear confused in their memory and thinking.

A constant slow rate is easy to catch on the electrocardiogram, making diagnosis simple. Optimistically, the slower the heart rate in a confused person, the more likely is the chance that an artificial pacemaker can measurably return the patient's mental function. The greater challenge in this area, however, is to capture the occasional, episodic slow heartbeat. These rarely are seen on a standard EKG machine, and may require a twenty-four-hour ambulatory EKG (called a Holtor monitor) for their detection. If mental confusion seems to come and go, it may take more than one monitor to establish with confidence that episodes of slow heartbeat are not causing episodes of confusion—all the more important since some doctors think that each episode of slow heartbeat and drop in brain circulation may leave a little bit of brain damage in its wake.

Beyond looking for slow heartbeats, the EKG performs a general check of the heart for signs of hardening of the arteries. Evidence on EKG of an old small heart attack doesn't necessarily prove that a person has small-stroke dementia, but it is not entirely irrelevant. Heart attacks are caused by hardening of the arteries to the heart (the process is technically known as atherosclerosis). There is not much difference between the arteries of the heart and those of the brain in terms of their vulnerability to hardening and narrowing by atherosclerosis. Evidence of a prior small heart attack may be circumstantial, but in a memory-impaired individual it does at least raise the likelihood that there may be some element of small-stroke disease present.

Chest X Ray: This is a time-honored part of every physical exam, and I suppose ought to be done. There are indeed some findings on the chest X ray that can explain an elderly person's intellectual failings. Most of these, however, are better revealed by the examination (heart valve problems limiting the flow of blood to the brain, for example, or chronic lung disease). When the chest X ray turns up a surprise diagnosis in a failing elderly person, the diagnosis is often something extremely depressing, like lung cancer. One small point to ask about, however, is whether the X ray shows any signs of old scars suggestive of childhood or adolescent TB infection. If it does, make special note of the next section.

Skin Testing: There are a few very odd infections of the brain that can given the appearance of dementia, but unlike Alzheimer's disease, these brain infections are curable. Syphilis is one, but this is diagnosed by the VDRL blood test mentioned earlier. The remaining possible infections include tuberculosis and an assortment of fungal infections (histoplasmosis, coccidiomycosis, criptospirosis). In the natural world, people who are exposed to these infections in their youth either die (which is very rare, unless they have AIDS) or suffer a mild illness from which they recover. Recovery, however, is not the same as complete elimination of tuberculosis germs or fungi from the body. Some few living organisms forever remain in the body, surrounded by scar tissue and kept in a state of suspended animation by the immune system.

But the immune system of older persons weakens over time, and on occasion some of these infections that have lain dormant for decades reawaken. Most times these old infections reawaken in the lung, but sometimes they activate in the brain, where they cause a very slow, smoldering form of tuberculosis or fungal meningitis. This kind of meningitis does not remotely look like the usual viral or bacterial types, with their high fevers, stiff necks, seizures, and coma. Fungal or tuberculosis meningitis can progress slowly for months, producing the changes of progressive dementia until finally diagnosed (possibly at autopsy). It is a rare but curable form of dementia, and one that ought to be kept in mind. Presently there is no blood test for any of these infections, but skin testing for signs of exposure to TB or the fungi can give a good clue—particularly if your parent grew up poor during the Depression or war years (TB), once lived in the Ohio–Mississippi valley (histoplasmosis), or traveled even briefly through the southwestern United States (coccidiomycosis).

If the skin test is positive, make certain that this fact is communicated to your neurologist. The only way to know for sure if the skin test means active brain infection will be a spinal tap, although the neurologist can give a good indication from physical examination whether a spinal tap actually is warranted. The phrase "spinal tap" tends to excite immediate fear in many people; everyone thinks they know somebody who knows somebody who was supposedly paralyzed by a spinal tap. This is one of those puzzling phantom stories that endure for decades but is not true. I know that I have never met that mythical person paralyzed by a spinal tap, and no doctor that I know ever met him or her. You also will never meet that individual. If any doctor whose judgment you trust suggests a spinal tap, I advise you to proceed immediately with the test. You can safely skip the angst and avoid having a major family conference on the matter.

EEG: A few years ago, an EEG (electroencephalogram) was an essential part of the diagnostic workup, and it may still have a minor place. It may be useful for diagnosing some rare types of epilepsy that may present with unusual seizures of the temporal lobe. Typically these seizures can present with sudden outbursts of violence, hallucination, or confusion. An EEG by itself should not be considered an essential first order of business. It can be done in conjunction with a neurologist's examination, there being little advantage to the test without the neurologist's input.

Head Scan: Within the past few years, the CAT scan (which uses a computer to analyze X rays and generate a picture of the brain) has been replaced by the MRI scan (which uses a computer to analyze a magnetic field and generate a picture of the brain). The MRI scan has several advantages over the CAT scan which make it the present-day instrument of choice in the diagnosis of dementia, but most importantly, the MRI can see smaller sites of small-stroke injury to the brain than can the CAT scan. The lack of exposure to X rays from an MRI is a minor but important consideration; the improved quality of the pictures is the real reason for its popularity.

Contrary to general opinion, neither the MRI nor the CAT scan can actually diagnose Alzheimer's disease. There is an incorrect notion that "atrophy" on one of these scans means that one has confirmed the presence of Alzheimer's disease. This error persists even among some doctors, because it is such a powerfully intuitive notion to equate the figurative "atrophy" of a person's mental functions with atrophic appearance of an older person's brain on the MRI or CAT scan.

This "logic," however, is wrong. The "atrophy of the brain" seen in old people on scanning their heads is mostly due to a loss of water and nonnerve tissue substance that occurs with normal aging. It is not a diagnostic sign of Alzheimer's disease.

When the CAT scan was new and few machines existed, old persons with dementia tended to have a high priority for access to the relatively scarce scanners, and consequently their heads were scanned far more often than were the heads of normal elderly persons. A false impression gained credence in the medical community that Alzheimer's disease could be "seen" on the scan as "atrophy of the brain." This error has not yet been entirely corrected in the minds of many doctors, even by the large number of CAT scan studies done in later years showing quite convincingly that the brains of normal elderly persons have the same amount of "atrophy" as do the brains of elderly persons with Alzheimer's disease.

In reality, the purpose of the head scan is not to diagnose Alzheimer's disease but to search for signs of other brain diseases that might be causing memory or behavioral abnormalities. As such, the scan remains an essential part of the diagnostic workup. Caution, however, needs to be advised in the interpretation of the scan results, and some of that caution needs to be maintained by you: *There is a sometimes irresistible tendency among patients, families, and doctors to assume that any abnormality found on a head scan must therefore be the cause of the person's problems.*

There are a variety of odd little abnormalities (small meningiomas, abnormal blood vessels, atrophy) that may have always resided in a person's brain—harmlessly—perhaps since birth or childhood. Since healthy persons rarely have scans, the existence of these "innocent bystanders" goes undetected. Their late discovery, at a time when the person is having mental difficulties, sometimes creates an almost irresistible bandwagon effect, in which there is a rush to place all the blame on whatever "abnormality" has been found. As the results of your parent's scan are discussed with you, be wary about what you are being told, and agree to no surgery without a second opinion.

With that caveat, then, the major objectives of the head scan are really to search for signs of the following illnesses that are *not* Alzheimer's disease:

Stroke: The appearance of a silent stroke in one of the areas that controls memory, personality, and movement can imitate Alzheimer's disease. Although there is no remedy for a completed stroke, this condition is relatively treatable, in the sense that medication affecting blood clotting may prevent future strokes. If future strokes can be averted, there is at least the hope that the memory and behavioral problems will not worsen over time as they do with Alzheimer's disease. Furthermore, since the brain never ceases its attempts to reroute information around a damaged area, there may over time even be some minor improvement in memory or behavior (the stress remaining on "minor").

Subdural Hematoma: Minor head trauma in the elderly can cause small blood vessels to rupture not in the brain itself but in the space between the surface of the brain and the dura, a thick leathery layer of grizzle that covers the brain. Rupture of these vessels can lead to an appreciable-sized blood clot that presses on the surface of the brain from above. Lightly pressed brain tissue does not die, but it does temporarily stop working, so that a subdural hematoma may display its presence indirectly—by causing malfunction of an area of underlying brain and giving the elderly person the appearance of dementia. Large clots causing severe pressure can be suctioned out by neurosurgery and the "dementia" reversed. Many clots, however, disappear by themselves, and many neurosurgeons prefer to watch and wait, nature and time doing a good job of reabsorbing many such clots. The caveat mentioned earlier applies here—just because a person has a small subdural does not mean that it is the cause of all mental conditions (Alzheimer's disease patients get subdurals too). No surgery should be performed without first obtaining a second opinion, unless the clot is very large and there is a question of life or death from the degree of pressure being applied to the brain.

Meningioma: A meningioma is a benign tumor that almost anywhere else in the body would be inconsequential. When it forms on the dura, the thick layer of grizzle surrounding the brain (mentioned above), these small tumors may cause pressure on the brain lying beneath it, very much like the subdural blood clots. Unlike the blood clots, however, which sometimes disappear by themselves, a meningioma can be removed only by surgery. Expert neurological and neurosurgical opinion again is needed here, because many meningiomas are in fact innocent bystanders, while some are in fact the culprit causing the dementia. If the meningioma is culpable, surgery may salvage a human mind. Often it happens that well-intentioned physicians perform surgery for a meningioma with high expectations, only to rediscover the lesson that even people with Alzheimer's disease can have a meningioma.

Brain cancer: Rarely will malignant brain tumors be found in the brain as the cause of dementia. Although brain cancer is on the top of the list of everyone's anxieties before the scan is done, it is rarely the cause of dementia that has persisted for one or two years. Brain cancer seldom gives a person that much time.

Normal pressure hydrocephalus: This is a very controversial entity, in which there is enlargement of the inner fluid chambers of the brain. It can produce a very profound dementia, the equal of any case of Alzheimer's disease. The dementia of NPH additionally has a special tendency to be associated very early on with significant difficulty walking and with loss of bladder control—both much earlier than is generally true with Alzheimer's disease. The perplexing part of NPH is that some cases get miraculously better with surgery—and some do not. Considerable frustrating effort has gone into trying to refine the criteria for successfully separating the one group from the other, sparing the latter needless surgery. Selection of the best candidates for surgery remains an imperfect science, however, although a prior history of meningitis, head trauma, or temporary improvement in memory after a spinal tap all seem to predict a more favorable response to the surgery.

Whether the discovery on head scanning is of a subdural blood clot, meningioma, or hydrocephalus, to some people the issue is moot, since for them the very word "neurosurgery" is unimaginable. Many sons and daughters feel with absolute conviction that they would never "subject" their parent to neurosurgery—period. Most of this fear is primitive and unscientific, resting entirely on vividly imagined ideas of what neurosurgery means. Without expecting to believed, let me assure you that elderly people tolerate neurosurgery better than abdominal surgery. It is simpler, less complicated (that's right), and far distant from the other vital organs most prone to postoperative complications. Although no surgery should be done without good reason, if the likelihood of improvement in a person's dementia exists and surgery is strongly predicted *by two neurosurgeons*, I would *strongly advise* taking the chance on the surgery, in hopes of averting the future catastrophic consequences of a progressive dementia.

Coming to market as this book is being written are several new diagnostic tests for Alzheimer's dementia. These include one blood test (called APO-E) and two tests that can only be performed on spinal fluid (Tau protein and A-beta 42). Although already available, they are only slowly coming into general use and will most likely be more readily available at Alzheimer's Disease Centers than through the offices of general physicians. The use of all three tests—APO-E, Tau and A-beta 42—in a demented person can predict whether the dementia definitely is or is not Alzheimer's dementia in about 60 percent of cases. As new drugs specifically for Alzheimer's dementia come to market in the next few years, it will become increasingly important in choosing drug therapy to know as far as possible whether your parent does in fact have Alzheimer's dementia.

The MRI scan of the head usually brings the medical-neurological investigation to its conclusion. What can one expect from all of these tests? Statistically, out of every 100 elderly persons with memory problems who complete all of the tests mentioned, between 15 and 30 will by this point have discovered an explanation for their memory problem that is *not* Alzheimer's disease or small-stroke disease, and will be involved in a treatment or therapy that would not have been possible if Alzheimer's disease or small-stroke disease had been simply assumed to be the problem. What of the remainder? For them, the disease causing their brain damage will be one (or possibly both) of the two major causes of dementia in America today:

- Alzheimer's disease
- Multiple-stroke disease

If your diagnostic intervention has been timely, neither of these two illnesses will as yet be severe. Although neither is curable, both are treatable to some degree. What you need to know about the early years of dementia is the subject of the next chapter.

One last issue remains after all of the diagnostic tests are completed: If dementia is present, should you tell your parent the truth?

This is especially troubling when the dementia is felt to be due to Alzheimer's disease, since Alzheimer's may be the only cause of dementia that your parent knows anything about— and generally what they know is frightening. Often, being told of Alzheimer's seems like being given a death sentence or the news that one is about to be discarded by society.

Despite these negative initial reactions, most specialists in the field strongly favor telling patients the truth, although in a supportive way. They point out that many persons with early dementia fear they are going "crazy" and are at least partly comforted that their problems have not been imaginary and have been diagnosed as a physical condition. They also stress that many people do, in fact, live for years with Alzheimer's dementia, and that the progression from earliest signs to advanced dementia may take ten or fifteen years. In addition, many persons with Alzheimer's dementia (perhaps a third) have several years during which their disease seems not to worsen but to remain on a fairly level plateau. And finally there is the hope, just now starting to be realized, that the tremendous amount of research into Alzheimer's disease will yield new drugs and therapies to help treat the disorder.

In addition to the management steps outlined for you in this book, it would be well to remember that the National Alzheimer's Association can provide information on newsletters, booklets, videos, and support groups designed *for your parent* as well as *for you*. A sense of community is slowly growing among individuals with early Alzheimer's dementia, with a growing circulation of poetry and art created by persons with early dementia. Ultimately the best way not to allow your mom or dad to surrender to hopelessness is to ensure that you do not either. It is not what you say but rather what you feel in your heart that will be communicated.

4

The Inner Workings
of a Failing Mind

THE MAJORITY OF ELDERLY PERSONS who display the warning signs of intellectual failure as discussed in chapter 2 will ultimately be found to have a dementing illness. The illness statistically will be either of the Alzheimer's disease type or of the small-stroke type. Under the microscope, these two disease are entirely dissimilar—and yet, as different as they are from each other, outwardly they produce the same appearance of "dementia," with almost indistinguishable problems of memory, mood, and behavior. Does it matter which one is the culprit in your parent?

Some would say not. They would argue that although Alzheimer's disease and small-stroke disease may be different under the microscope, in their ultimate effects on a person's life, they might just as well be considered identical. After all, each is so common among the elderly as to be endemic, and in fact so common that there is a good chance that an older person with dementia might be suffering from both at the same time! Neither one is a curable disease, and inasmuch as each disease produces the same kinds of problems for patient and family, one could very well write a textbook for the care of demented persons and never have to change one bit of management advice according to whether Alzheimer's disease or small-stroke disease was the causative illness.

Strengthening the argument of those doctors who would lump the two together is the fact that there is no entirely reliable way to separate cases of Alzheimer's disease from cases of small-stroke disease in life. After death the distinction is simple, and if brain biopsy were not such a drastic measure, it would be possible to diagnose the two reliably before death. At the current state of knowledge, any decision to call one person's dementia Alzheimer's disease and another's small-stroke disease is always guesswork and always based on the circumstantial evidence discussed below.

Such indifference to diagnostic accuracy may be a thing of the past in the near future, given the broad push of drug companies to develop drugs for Alzheimer's disease. Nevertheless, the amazing thing about brain diseases is that as far as a person's behavior is concerned, it matters not the method by which an area of brain is damaged, but simply what function that damaged part controlled.

Consider, for example, an area of the brain called temporal lobe. The temporal lobe plays a major role in memory, and injury to a person's temporal lobe will lead to short-term memory loss. The actual manner of injury is almost irrelevant. Whether it is pressure damage by a tumor, circulation cutoff by a stroke, an infectious abscess, hemorrhage from a ruptured blood vessel, or trauma from a bullet, the bottom line is that if the nerve cells of the temporal lobe are dead, the memories they held are gone. And of course, each of the families of each person whose temporal lobe was damaged by whatever means will be coping with a loved one with the same basic problems that come about from poor memory.

So too with Alzheimer's disease and small-stroke disease. Though they are two entirely different diseases under the microscope, the effects they produce in a person's life are almost identical. Each in its own different way causes very tiny areas of damage to the brain. Those areas of damage, initially so small and so widely separate, accumulate over time to cause progressive and widespread damage. In the early stages of both small-stroke disease and Alzheimer's disease, when the number of damaged brain areas is relatively small, the effects on brain function are subtle and confined to the higher abstract functions of the human brain.

As the damaged areas become more numerous, so too does the profundity of dysfunction in the person's memory and rational ability. Ultimately the damage in either disease will extend to areas that control balance, walking, coordination, and eating. Understandably, it may matter little to patient or family whether all of this is due to Alzheimer's disease damage or small-stroke disease damage; speculation quickly fades into the background as the task of coping with the brain-damaged behavior becomes paramount.

What, then, is the purpose for knowing or caring whether your parent has Alzheimer's disease or small-stroke disease? The answer for me lies in several points:

First, I believe that there is a small but sufficient divergence of treatments available now for the two diseases which warrants making some effort at distinction. At the time of this writing, I treat patients differently depending on whether I feel that either small-stroke disease or Alzheimer's disease is dominant in their case. Of course, without having a brain biopsy, neither I nor any other doctor can be *absolutely* certain if a person's dementia is either small-stroke or Alzheimer's disease, although small clues can be helpful. One clue is that persons who have lots of hardening of the arteries elsewhere in the body—heart disease or circulatory problems in the legs, for example—are statistically more likely to have small-stroke disease. A history of hypertension or cigarette smoking also increases the odds of small-stroke disease being the major problem. Alzheimer's disease tends to cause a smooth and progressive decline in a person's intellectual function, while small-stroke disease tends to be a bit more erratic, with periods of stability interrupted by periods of more rapid decline, presumably these being the days or weeks when the small-strokes are occurring. Hopefully soon the distinction between Alzheimer's disease and small-stroke disease will be more soundly scientific, with blood and spinal fluid tests soon to come on the market for the specific purpose of diagnosing Alzheimer's disease. At the present time, however, much can still be made of an educated physician's inferences about which disease is causing an individual's dementia.

I favor specific treatments for those patients in whom I feel a strong sense about the presence of either Alzheimer's disease or small-stroke disease. These measures include:

For Small-Stroke Disease:

- control of high cholesterol, with diet as well as medication
- cessation of smoking
- low doses of aspirin (80 milligrams per day, the equal of one children's strength) combined with Persantine (75 milligrams twice daily) to reduce blood microclotting
- vitamin E (400 units per day)
- fish oil capsules, twice daily, for an adjunct inhibition of blood clotting
- calcium tablets, approximately 500 to 650 milligrams each, twice daily, and two multivitamins a day, to minimize future skeletal calcium loss in anticipation of future walking problems and a higher risk of falling

For Alzheimer's Disease:

- a trial of Cognex, the only currently approved drug for the improvement of memory in patients with Alzheimer's disease. It is far from a miracle cure, as families will admit, yet sometimes small but wonderful improvements in overall function can occur with the drug. Because the drug can have side effects, many doctors are timid about its use, but if I feel a patient truly has Alzheimer's disease, I will aggressively push the dose to the maximal tolerable amount, the medication frequently not being effective unless it is used with boldness.

- calcium and multivitamins, in the same dose as for small-stroke disease and for the same reasons.

Will either of these programs "cure" their respective disease, small-stroke disease or Alzheimer's disease? Absolutely not! Would all doctors agree upon these same choices? Again not. From my own experience, I believe that there is good theoretical evidence to support the observation that small-stroke disease can be *slowed* (and perhaps for some time stopped) in its progression by these steps, and for Alzheimer's disease a higher degree of intellectual performance can often be achieved with the use of Cognex. Particularly in small-stroke disease, where the goal of medical treatment is to slow down or stabilize the disease's progression, there is a premium in starting treatment as early as possible, in the hope of salvaging as much brain function as possible.

The second point is that new treatments for either disease may develop in the short term. Certainly, if you live in hope and read newspapers or watch TV, you might want to have some idea of whether a new treatment being announced for either Alzheimer's disease or small-stroke disease may be of personal value to your mother or father. (In general, however, the imprecision of most news outlets for dementia is such that any news of an advancement would likely be announced under the more well known Alzheimer's disease regardless of its specificity for that particular type of dementia.)

Finally, I believe that it is entirely possible that knowing the likelihood that your parent has either Alzheimer's disease or small-stroke disease may have some practical importance for you as well.

Of course, it is true that knowing your parent has genuine Alzheimer's disease will not allow you to do much more than worry about your own future. Most children of patients with Alzheimer's disese already know from the popular media that the risk of Alzheimer's disease is higher in the children of patients with the disorder. Few know, however, that the risk is not as great as the media often make it appear. The highest risk for inheriting Alzheimer's occurs in those relatively rare cases when the disease hits a parent in their forties or fifties. In these families, the risk to future generations is indeed sobering. Most of the Alzheimer's disease in the population, however, affects much older persons, in their seventies or eighties. The older your parent is at the time of diagnosis, the *less* significant is your future risk, and indeed for cases of very late onset, in the upper eighties or the nineties, there is probably no increased risk for that patient's children compared to the rest of the population.

The dementia of small-stroke disease, however, may be a more escapable fate. There is no purely genetic risk here. Rather, the risk for small-stroke disease is associated with hypertension, smoking, and hypercholesterolemia. Witnessing the tragedy of your parent's life being decimated by small-stroke disease might provide a compelling motivation for a son or daughter to undertake a radical change in lifestyle.

As mentioned earlier, at the present time the diagnosis of Alzheimer's disease or small-stroke disease in a living individual rests upon a preponderance of circumstantial evidence and the physician's intuition. The likelihood of small-stroke disease is favored if

- there are other circulatory ailments affecting the heart, kidneys, or legs
- there is a past history of hypertension
- there is a past history of high cholesterol
- there is a past history of smoking
- the MRI scan shows large amounts of small spots consistent with vascular damage to the brain (called T-2 lesions)
- the dementia progresses with a an erratic, sputtering course, in which were periods of stability are punctuated by periods of deterioration when small strokes are taking place

A probable diagnosis of Alzheimer's disease is made if

- there is surprisingly little evidence of vascular disease elsewhere in the body
- the MRI scan is entirely without signs of unusual vascular-type lesions
- mental deterioration has been smooth and steadily progressive

There is still debate in the scientific community about the relative contributions of Alzheimer's disease and small-stroke disease to the total pool of individuals with dementia. In the late sixties, small-stroke disease was felt to be predominant; in the seventies and eighties, the estimates were revised to suggest that Alzheimer's disease was the major contributor. At the present time, the scientific pendulum seems to be swinging toward a compromise, suggesting that among groups of demented individuals, there are three roughly equal groups:

- About one third of people with dementia probably have pure Alzheimer's disease.
- About one third probably have only small-stroke disease.
- About one third have a mixture of both small-stroke disease and Alzheimer's disease, which is not so surprising given that both conditions are very common.

From a research scientist's point of view, this breakdown is troubling, especially the theory that as many as a third of the cases of dementia have two simultaneous diseases causing the dementia. This last third virtually guarantees that any treatment for either Alzheimer's disease or small-stroke disease is going to appear a bit paltry when the studies are done, always seeming to help only a minority of persons with dementia.

Why? Because those in the "mixed" group will continue to deteriorate from one disease process even if the other is halted completely. Imagine a theoretical "cure" for Alzheimer's disease being tested in the population. Given the prevalence of pure Alzheimer's disease, even a curative treatment would only appear to benefit about 30 percent of the subjects. The remaining two thirds would continue to deteriorate, being either partly or totally afflicted with small-stroke disease!

Even more perplexing is the case of an individual patient in such a study. If the person being treated with the magical cure for Alzheimer's disease were to continue to decline, should the treatment be abandoned? If one were certain that this patient was a case of pure small-stroke disease, it would make sense to stop the therapy, but not being certain, one is left to wonder whether the rate of worsening would have been even faster without the treatment. It is easy to imagine that a hypothetical "cure" for one type of dementia-causing disease would be applied to every person with dementia, even though only a third of those people would actually be helped by it.

Attempting to dramatically influence the course of dementia in even a third of patients is a pipe dream at this point in history. Yet, as the future develops, some advantage may exist to knowing as precisely as possible the actual cause of your parent's dementia. New scientific breakthoughs can be more rationally evaluated if you understand what type of dementia these breakthroughs are meant to help, and whether it is the type of dementing disease that your parent has.

In the everyday world of symptom management, however, it is unlikely to matter much what kind of disease process has caused your parent's dementia. The problems of dementia remain the same, regardless of the name of the disease causing the dementia, and the solutions also work equally well. For the next few chapters, I will not distinguish between small-stroke disease and Alzheimer's disease. From here on, we will use the general, noncommittal term "dementia" to reinforce the universality of everyday problem management. In terms of practical, day-to-day difficulties, the problems of small-stroke disease and Alzheimer's disease are the same and interchangeable.

Short-Term Memory Loss

In chapter 2, we discussed the kinds of early failures of memory, socialization, and numerical capability that are usually present for months to years before children admit to themselves their concern about Mom or Dad. These early problems are of importance for what they foretell of the future, but with the exception of not paying the utility bills, the early symptoms of dementia may still coexist with the ability of your parent to remain at home and independent. As time progresses, however, the changes in memory and behavior more typical of small-stroke disease or Alzheimer's disease will begin to surface on a permanent basis. The focus of this chapter is to explain in greater detail the mechanics of the memory difficulties that afflict a person during the early year or two with small-stroke disease or Alzheimer's disease, and how to cope with them.

The memory loss in Alzheimer's disease and small-stroke disease almost exclusively affect *short-term* memory. Short-term memory is an inherently more fragile memory storage system of the brain, where images of the past few seconds, minutes, hours, days, or weeks are stored in a volatile memory bank. At all ages of life, only a fraction of a person's short-term memory ever gets rewritten into the relatively more secure long-term memory. What fraction is selected for long term recall is surprisingly variable. Making a conscious effort to remember helps, but only a small amount, as a review of high school math or history may illustrate.

More effective than the desire to remember is the association of a short-term memory with a simultaneous emotional stimulus (whether pleasant or not); the emotional overtone seems to enhance the likelihood that our brains will prod their memory systems into making a permanent record. Curiously, sometimes a random short-term memory is recorded indelibly, but for no clear reason. Most people can recall throughout their lives a few "scenes" from about age two—they may remember sitting in their highchair or re-collect a particular picture on the nursery wall. Why one moment is selected from all the others to be transcribed into permanent memory remains a mystery.

The way in which short-term memory is lost is very curious. The most recent memories are the ones we lose first. Early on in the disease, a person may only have difficulty remembering what was said or done five minutes ago but have fairly good access to all other memory function. As the disease progresses, however, this memory "blind spot" begins to enlarge. At first it may be only the past day or two that cannot be recalled, but as time goes by, this becomes the past few weeks...then months...then years. The technical name for this process is *retrograde amnesia*, and it forces a person's mental frame of reference for all decisions and actions ever further into their own personal past, creating ever more potential for a mismatch between their personal view of "reality" and everyone else's idea of "reality."

Persons with small-stroke disease or Alzheimer's disease may nevertheless continue to have good long-term memory until late in the disease. For many years, they can remain very adept at remembering details from twenty or thirty years ago. The memories from five minutes ago, however, often seem to randomly disappear. It is important to realize that even with retrograde amnesia, persons with dementia may not be totally unable to recall recent events, but that they clearly have tremendous difficulty in this area. Patients with Alzheimer's disease or small-stroke disease may retain some short-term memories even if they cannot hold on to most. For example, they are better able to remember their own questions from five minutes ago than they are to remember your answers.

This discrepancy between the memory for questions and the memory for answers creates a cycle of repetitiveness. "What time do we leave?" may be asked, answered, and asked again every five minutes. The periodicity of this cycle varies slightly from person to person and may reflect the chemical "life expectancy" of short-term memory in the absence of some further next processing step.

Why questions are remembered and the answers forgotten is not clear, although the explanation may not be mysterious. Perhaps by definition, the questions remembered are merely the questions that the person *has* in fact remembered; you will not be asked the questions they have forgotten. Yet it appears that the questions recalled by the demented person are seldom random, but usually have an undercurrent of anxiety attached to them. What time to leave or what time the others arrive—perhaps even in dementia the association of an emotion with memory helps to stabilize the thought in the mind. Sadly, no comparable way of cementing a reassuring response into memory seems to exist.

Readers familiar with computers may notice a crude similarity between human short-term memory and a computer's RAM, and between long-term memory and a computer's hard drive. Cognizant of the simplicity of such a comparison, it may be helpful to consider short-term memory loss to be a defective RAM system that suffers from erratic write/read failure. Long-term memory would, by analogy, exist as the biological equivalent of the computer's hard disk. Dementia in its early stages damages the RAM of short-term memory; only later does it begin to erase the hard disk of long-term memory, starting with the most recent memory "files" and working backward in time to erase progressively older and older memory.

Repetitiveness is one of the most frustrating and aggravating experiences that derive from dementia. Typically it drives family members to the point of exasperation, for which afterward most sons or daughters confess feeling ashamed of themselves. Do not feel guilty if you find yourself on the verge of losing patience or becoming irritated. Almost all family members do, and they too feel badly about themselves for reacting that way. In considering repetitiveness, it is tempting to suspect that the behavior is a willful device to gain attention or to annoy you, or that it could be overcome if your parent would just pay attention and *try* to remember, but all of this is false. The real explanation for repetitiveness is the following "formula" by which a demented mind operates:

Memory Loss + Anxiety = Search for Reassurance

If you can comprehend the impact of this equation, it will allow you to break into your parent's demented mind and will point the way to solutions not only to the question-answer cycle of repetitiveness but also to a variety of other "confused" behaviors. In the absence of any ability to improve the person's memory, to break the cycle you need to reach the anxiety. It is beyond the ability of most persons with dementia to explain their anxiety to you directly, so in part you need to make an imaginative guess as to the cause.

Short-term memory loss is also part of another important equation that will dictate the mental life of your parent with early dementia:

Memory Loss + Human Logic = Confusion

Although much about the behavior of a demented person appears, at first glance, to be bizarre, it is, in fact, entirely logical. Only the premise of a demented person's behavior is in error. If you accept the demented person's frame of reference, the remainder of what they say and do is perfectly logical.

For example, put yourself in the place of your father with dementia for a moment, and share for a moment his frame of reference. *If, indeed, the year were 1955, then would it not also be true that*

- this "old woman" in his bedroom could not possibly be the girl he married ten years ago after he came home from the service;
- the familiarity of this older woman living in his home would suggest that she must be his mother;

- all these people about him are certainly too old to be his own children; is he at someone else's house?
- everyone here is very nice, but it's daylight out, and it's time to get back to work before the boss finds he's gone;
- now its dark, and these people have been trying to persuade him to stay all day; he's been gracious in agreeing to do so, but he is starting to get a bit annoyed with them. It's late, and it's time to go home now; his wife and kids will be starting to worry if they don't hear from him by this hour.

The point of this imaginary exercise is to remind you that the only difference between the workings of *your* mind and that of your "ill" parent is that you and your parent do not share the same point of reference. It is only the *first* premise that is in error with a failing parent. Beyond that first incorrect assessment of the situation, the powers of rationality and logic survive to a surprising degree. It is not "nonsense" that your parent appears to speak, but a different "sense." If you are to be successful in avoiding the use of drugs for every little problem, you will need to cut loose your own imagination and seek to enter into the imaginative time and place from which your parent is viewing the present. If successful, you may frequently get to the root contradictions between personal and public reality and help eliminate some of the "confusion."

There is one last "equation" to help understand the mental life of a person with dementia, and that is described below:

$$\frac{\text{Long-Term Memory Recall}}{\text{Short-Term Memory Loss}} = \text{Depression}$$

Of course, depression was first discussed in the context of true clinical depression as a possible sole cause of behavioral malfunction in your parent. True depression can imitate dementia by the process of "pseudo memory loss." If the advice in chapter 3 was taken, this question of depression as the single cause of memory loss and social withdrawal should have already been considered and presumably was replaced by the diagnosis of dementia.

But proving that dementia and not depression is the cause of a person's intellectual failure does not eliminate depression as an issue to deal with. Your parent with dementia is still, in fact, subject to becoming depressed, as the equation above suggests. This tendency for persons with dementia to become depressed tends to occur in the early stages of dementia. In the early stages, short-term memory loss is slight and long-term recollection is great, leaving a large potential for depression as the difference between the way things are (and are going) can be compared to the way things were.

This formula is deliberately written as a fraction to remind the reader that a large product (depression) can be generated by the combination of a large numerator (good long-term memory recall) with a small denominator (slight short-term memory loss). Herein is contained one of the continuing problems in medical diagnostics: In *very early* dementia, the associated depression may be so great as to make it extremely difficult to distinguish "demented depression" from "true depression."

That early dementia would be associated with depression according to this simple equation would likely appear as reasonable to most readers. It is easy to empathize with the situation and to imagine that the knowledge that one has Alzheimer's disease would be profoundly depressing, and that with enough insight into themselves and their growing intellectual disability, anyone with early dementia would become understandably depressed by that vision.

Perhaps the mystery is less why some patients with early dementia become depressed than it is why so many persons with dementia do not! Clearly there are other factors involved besides the "logical" development of depression as one begins to fail. Why depression occurs in one person and not another is not entirely well understood. Although universal agreement does not exist on this issue, several observations about demented persons suggest that there may be a difference in susceptibility to depression according to whether the cause of the dementia is Alzheimer's disease or small-stroke disease.

Persons with Alzheimer's disease have a conspicuous tendency to ignore their own failings. Even with early short-term memory loss, they can display an astonishing degree of general inattention to memory problems early in their dementia. Persons who still possess a large amount of retained memory, who might be expected to be at the greatest risk for depression, may show inexplicable tolerance and self-forgiveness of their own memory failings!

In contrast, persons with small-stroke disease have been long suspect to be more susceptible to depression. This suspicion rests in part on observations of people with large strokes. Large-stroke disease is the familiar picture of a person having a stroke—the sudden appearance of a paralyzed arm or leg, with possible difficulty either in forming or understanding speech. Such big, obvious stroke disease is very different from small-stroke disease, but the two share some interesting features. For example, it has been learned that persons who have had a large stroke almost always have a period of depression for three to six months afterward. One might assume that this is only logical—when a stroke is large and leaves part of the body paralyzed, one could still argue that it is the sense of loss that creates the psychological experience of depression.

And yet this appears to be a too simple explanation, since even persons whose strokes occur in one of the "silent" areas of the brain and who suffer no paralysis still seem to show the same degree of poststroke depression. There is evidence that the brain responds to injury with depression, whether the injury is large or small. Once triggered, this poststroke depression has a life of its own. If true, this observation would suggest that persons with small-stroke disease may be particularly susceptible to depression during the early stages of their illness, and that the cause of their depression may be more "biological" than "logical."

At times, it is not easy to separate true depression from demented depression. This is why it is not infrequent in the elderly for a successfully treated depression to be followed in a few years by dementia, a pattern that is not seen in young persons with depression. When depression first appears late in life, it may just be depression—or it may be that the depression being triggered is more obvious than the small, silent strokes triggering it. As with cancer patients who seem "cured" for a few years only to suffer a devastating relapse, any "cure" of an elderly person with depression needs to be followed by a period of heightened watchfulness.

Whatever the nature of your parent's depression— whether it is true depression or the depression that associates with early dementia—one thing is important to keep in mind:

Depression is always treatable

It may not be *curable* unless it is "true depression," but it is always *treatable* and should always be treated for several important reasons:

- Depression is an unpleasant state of mind, whatever the cause. It is psychic suffering and deserves to be eased for this reason if none other.
- As poorly as a demented person will perform a given task, that task will be done *even more poorly* if the demented person is also depressed and thereby lacking in motivation and desire to do their best.
- Depression magnifies all problems, including the perceived suffering of arthritic aches and pains.
- Depression is associated with problems of motivation, behavior, appetite, sleep, and bowels, and these problems may not improve unless the depression is adequately treated.

   The presence of depression in a demented person does have one silver lining—it implies that the dementia is not yet so terrible. The act of being depressed requires a fair amount of brain power, and consequently a depressed and demented individual must be presumed to still have a significant amount of underlying mental function even if things on the surface appear terrible. The presence of depression offers some promise that if the depression can be alleviated, there may be the reappearance of a considerable amount of brain function that had been presumed lost.

   Depression is therefore always treatable, even if it is coexisting with dementia. This warrants intervention for the depression, an issue on which all specialists on dementia agree. The treatment of depression itself is outside the focus of this book, but the following advisories are worth noting:

- Depression, whether true depression or associated with dementia, is a real, biological, physical disorder of the brain. Psychotherapy, counseling, behavior therapy, and other types of treatment by talking may be good for the soul, but they will *not* substitute for medical treatment. One cannot persuade or distract a person from being depressed by talk or socialization, any more than one could use these tactics to alter the course of a person with pneumonia.

- Drug treatment is very effective for depression and should be chosen by a psychiatrist or geriatrician familiar with treatment of the elderly. Older persons with or without dementia frequently require lower doses of antidepressant drugs than are commonly given to younger depressed persons. Even more important is the fact that older persons often have serious complications if they are given the "normal" dose of an antidepressant drug. Many prominent and expensive psychiatrists do not treat a large number of elderly persons in their practice for many reasons, including skimpy Medicare reimbursement, prejudice against the elderly, or prejudice by the elderly against psychiatry in general. Be sure that the psychiatrist is very familiar with older patients.

- Electroshock therapy (ECT) is safe and effective. Present-day ECT bears no similarity to horror stories from the 1930's and 1940's. Unilateral ECT is safely administered under light sedation and, done correctly, is both *more successful* and *safer* for the body than many antidepressant drugs. The memory loss it produces is temporary and wears off after a few days, and ECT should not bear the stigma it does. Although few persons ever believe these facts, it should be clearly understood that if drug therapy has been tried and has failed, ECT is definitely to be chosen before abandoning a person, demented or not, to the psychic pain of depression.

The equation for depression does hold one last remaining insight into the workings of the demented mind:

$$\frac{\text{Long-Term Memory Recall}}{\text{Short-Term Memory Loss}} = \text{Depression}$$

As dementia progresses, long-term recall will erode and there will be a loss of intellectual power. As dementia worsens, depression becomes less and less a problem. The extension of retrograde amnesia further and further into the past erases the recollection of the former self; the point of reference begins to fade, as memories of independence, family, job, and achievement begin to disappear. Ironically, the worsening of dementia may serve as nature's ultimate salve to a troubled, depressed, and hurting mind.

The Loss of Language

Short-term memory loss is only one of the two major, crippling dysfunctions to afflict the brain of a demented person. The other, arguably the worse of the pair, is the loss of language. Much of the anger, rage, frustration, and agitation of dementia is attributable to the inability of the demented person to communicate feelings, as well as the inability of the family and caregivers to use words to convey intent, purpose, and reassurance.

Discussion of language almost immediately suggests verbal language, the ability to speak and understand. In actuality, a close inspection of language function reveals that there are several separate but interwoven functions of language that harmonize in human communication. These include

- knowing what you mean to communicate
- the ability to speak words
- remembering the meanings which have been assigned to words
- understanding the spoken words of others
- being able to write
- being able to understand the written words of others

All of these functions appear to be carried out by different parts of the brain, although all of these parts lie very close to each other. Ultimately, all will be lost to dementia, but for several years you may discover that some functions do not work but that others still do. A written question may be understood; the same question spoken may be received by your parent's brain as indecipherable gibberish. Similarly, if the meanings of words are being lost, you may attune your ears not to the exact words spoken by your parent, but the category from which your parent is choosing. Your parent may repeat the word "car" while at the doctor's office, but by loosening your associations, you might correctly guess that the real intent is to get back into the car and go home.

The loss of language function imposes several constraints on the workings of a demented mind, and those are worth learning. As language is lost, one can note a tendency toward the following:

- reliance upon nonverbal body language, facial expression, and tone of voice to guess the speaker's meaning and intentions
- inability to follow the meaning of complex, multipart sentences
- inability to comprehend sentences in the subjective or conditional tenses, and greater reliance upon simple, concrete statements
- reliance in conversation upon stereotypical phrases

The uneven pattern in which the individual steps of language processing are lost can create interesting combinations. Some individuals are able to speak sentences fluently and with clear diction while having no idea of what they themselves are saying. Others can understand your words and will nod correctly to questions, but may be virtually mute in terms of being able to speak their answers. Strange subsets of language may be preserved. Genteel, polite individuals may be left with a vocabulary consisting of rude language embarrassing to their families. Immigrants invariably tend to lose the use of their acquired English language but will preserve their mother tongue for much longer periods of time.

People who can no longer speak words can often be induced to sing lyrics by playing the appropriate music. Music, it seems, is processed, stored, and recalled by the brain in an entirely different manner than other language functions, and this phenomenon can sometimes be used to open avenues of communciation when that of language has become effectively closed off.

There are rare cases of isolated short-term memory loss due to local trauma to the brain. These persons live their lives in an eternal present. It is a debilitating affliction, but even these rare cases are not as incapacitating as the additional burden sustained by the dementia patient by their loss of the ability to communicate abstractly via language.

— 5

When the Going Gets Tough

SOME EXTRAORDINARY FAMILIES are able to deny the existence of a dementia in their loved one for five or six years, but the average family will admit the presence of dementia after approximately one or two years from the appearance of the earliest signs. In the life of a family, dementia exists when practical activities of daily living are being repeatedly affected by intellectual failure. Without supervision, the safety of your parent will at this point be felt to be reasonably threatened. The area of perceived threat varies. The initial issue may be weight loss, malnutrition, poor hygiene, neglect of medical care due to poor compliance with medication, or the imminent danger of wandering or fire.

These are emotionally tough years, because they represent a particularly difficult combination of what has been lost and what remains of the individual's persona. In very early dementia, your parent's willpower and desire to be independent can be more easily indulged, since the problem areas of dysfunction are relatively minor. In very late dementia, the management problems are major, but the disease is so advanced that your parent's willpower will not be an issue. But in the middle stage of dementia, you confront a double challenge. The problems from the dementia will now touch upon key areas of living. Increasingly you will feel yourself under pressure to intervene, but there will likely remain enough of your parent's sense of independence to obstruct your efforts.

Do not think that your parent is alone in this. The typical person with dementia will never acknowledge an inability to handle their own lives. If they acknowledge any difficulty at all they invariably consider it minor. Usually they will attempt to turn the tables on the entire issue and may accuse their children of being oversolicitous, overly concerned, or of even "smothering" them.

Dementia may be destroying the inner core of a person's intellectual function, but a lifetime of long-established behavioral patterns leaves an outer shell of personhood. For some time, this shell may continue to possess all of the familiar attributes of your parent, including their expectation of your deference to their authority. By the time that dementia is interfering with daily living, however, you may trust that this familiar appearance has become more show than substance.

Because they are becoming genuinely less capable, demented persons become very rigid and resistant to change. Change of any kind requires adaptation and mental agility, and these are precisely the kinds of intellectual skills that are in critically short supply. Change becomes the threat to be avoided at all costs. Demented persons very acutely sense that if they attempt to cope with new situations or environments, they will be exposed. The response of a demented parent, therefore, to almost any suggestion of change is invariably the same: "No!"

You will be less perplexed by your parent's refusal of your efforts if you understand from the onset that the merit of your suggestion is never an issue, but rather that you are asking your parent to *change* part of their established pattern of life. Do you want to have "Meals on Wheels" because mom clearly can no longer cook dinner and is losing weight? Do you want to help hire a maid to clean the house once or twice a week? Are you willing to visit weekly and lay out the medication on a schedule? Pose any question that implies a constructive suggestion to a particular problem, and it can be said beforehand that the answer will be no.

The perception of change as threat finds a natural ally in the typical demented person's relative blindness to their own memory problems. For example, your suggestion will be even less acceptable if it implies paying money. Because of retrograde memory loss, the value of money undergoes a process of psychological deflation. Hiring a nurse or attendant for fifteen dollars an hour will be viewed in the context of hourly wages of ten, twenty, or thirty years ago, and your parent will probably be genuinely staggered at the outrageous cost. This mention of money is often the coup de grâce to any home care suggestion. Your parent's refusal will be presented as the judgment of a fiscally more prudent parent still looking out for their profligate offspring.

As Humpty Dumpty points out to Alice in *Through the Looking Glass*, "The question is, which is to be master—that's all." Before considering the next few chapters, you will need to establish in your own mind who, between your demented parent and yourself, is to be in charge. This is a pivotal moment in both of your lives. That test will come when your suggestions are refused. Which of you will prevail? You know better than your parent that their willpower is just a shell that cannot stand up to your own force of will, should you choose to exert that will. But is it right to do so? Is it better to respect your parent's wishes and thereby preserve this kindly fiction of independence, or has the time come for you to push through your parent's resistance as if through a hollow eggshell? You must either stay your parent's child or become your parent's parent.

There is no absolute answer as to whether it is right and proper to stand uninvited at the helm of another's life. Nor does one best time exist when it can be done without pain. Some parents, by their lifelong personality style, make the role reversal easier than others. It is comparatively easier to take over the life of a constitutionally congenial or passive person, compared with someone who lived a strong, independent, and dominating existence. Children of the latter often have become deeply ingrained with feelings of awe or even intimidation by a parent who defined the child's role in family dynamics. Such forceful parents, even when demented, consider themselves still the natural ruler of the family. Even as adults, children will find it distressing to attempt to intervene in their parent's life from an historical perspective of submissiveness.

Some children never do take this step—they never do push through the shell of their demented parent's will. In some cases, the urge to do so is simply not strong enough to override their childhood role. They remain as paralyzed spectators to the inevitable consequences of a demented person's insistence upon complete independence in the face of worsening mental dysfunction. These children may continue their attempts to help their parent cope with problems, but they accomplish little in a setting where their demented parent retains the ultimate right of decision.

Other offspring refuse to take the step of becoming their parent's parent, but do so quite deliberately. With no doubt about their ability to assert control if desired, some children consciously make a value judgment allowing their parent to have the full illusion of independence and autonomy regardless of the consequences. They do not doubt the consequences, which are predictably weight loss, sickness, injury, and death. Rather, they may contemplate a parent who throughout life savored such independence that both parent and child are prepared to have life end rather than to surrender its meaning.

To love a parent does not presuppose any one "right" or "wrong" decision. Any decision is "right" if it represents the best of which you are capable, and if it is congruent with your parent's life and philosophy.

In the reality of life, however, most children do at some point come to believe they now have reasons of pressing urgency for intervening in a deteriorating situation. And for them, ultimately there is only one solution, and that is to take action. At that point, you no longer ask your demented parent's approval or permission to act, but you offer them only as much voice and opinion as you can in what is going to happen. It may be home care, or Meals on Wheels; it may be nursing home placement or a doctor's appointment. Whatever you have come to decide needs to be done now will be done—calmly, kindly, and with a soothing reassurance in your voice. If your parent deals with surprises poorly, you involve them as much as possible in the planning; if anticipation brings anxiety, you keep your own counsel and present them with the fully realized situation.

You wouldn't ask your toddler to agree to a measles vaccination; you wouldn't cancel the appointment or turn around and go home if the child said no. Fundamentally, of course, you have no doubts about your responsibility to care for your child, and no one doubts your responsibility outweighs your young child's earnest opinions. In dementia, the fundamental issue is the same—ultimately, who is in charge. These decisions seldom lend themselves to consensus building. The gulf in perspective between a healthy and a demented mind is so great as to preclude agreement between them.

Consciously, almost every child of a demented parent knows that the moral right is on their side, but many remain in a state of emotional conflict because they cannot help but be hurt by their parent's words of anger. It helps a bit to keep in mind that the words are not really being spoken by your parent but by their disease, rising up in your parent's voice. Nevertheless, so emotionally bound are parent and child that there is no mind technique that can completely shield the child's emotional center from the stress of confrontation with their own mother or father. And when the focus of the parent's anger is genuine hurt at the child's perceived ingratitude, greed or meanness, the burden of guilt can be nearly too much to bear.

Salvation comes, ironically, from the dementia. After so much anger and bluff, most children are amazed at the rapidity with which the typical demented parent will cease to argue. This is particularly true of home attendants. The placement of a "stranger" into your parent's home is the issue most likely to arouse emotional fireworks. And yet once the worker is in place, it is surprising how quickly many demented persons will accept the worker—often in a matter of days or weeks. Memory loss can ease management problems at times, as the memory of life *before* the worker's arrival slips away and the present situation becomes the norm. Ironically, it may only be a short time before the once hated worker becomes so integrated into your parent's life that any absence on weekends or holidays becomes a source of anxiety!

In dealing with the problems of dementia, this pattern will become familiar. The change that is so fiercely resisted fairly quickly turns into the new status quo to be defended. Your parent will rarely complain to you about a problem. You will recognize yourself that a problem exists, either because you see it with your own eyes or because of the complaints of home care workers, friends, or neighbors. At that point, you may solicit your parent's opinion, but you will not ask your parent's permission to set about solving the problem. You may choose to act or not to act, but the responsibility will be yours. If the decision is to act, you will not expect approval or gratitude except in the ultimate results.

If this advice appears harsh, remind yourself that it is not inconsistent with love. Rather, this is the dark side of love, which is called responsibility. Your heart may break, but your will must not.

6

Helping a Failing Mind

THE PROBLEMS DISCUSSED in the next three chapters have a common denominator—they are all prevalent in moderately severe dementia. Happily, experience suggests that no one individual will display every problem discussed here. Nevertheless, these problems put your parent at risk for suffering, sickness, injury, and death. If not solved, they will cause home care workers to quit or may so stress the family as to lead to the estrangement of siblings or to the premature placement of your parent into a nursing home.

Although nursing homes have a legitimate and valuable place in the care of demented persons, the institutionalization of a demented parent is often done too quickly and for the wrong reasons. With more effective problem solving earlier in the course of their decline, many of today's nursing home residents might still be with family, surrounded by the people and homes for whom they worked all their lives. By making an effort to cope with behavioral problems as soon as they appear, a son or daughter can often stabilize the home situation before it has deteriorated beyond redemption, and thereby win additional years for their mom or dad to live with a sense of belonging.

In each of the discussions that follow, an attempt has been made to present nondrug management strategies first and to reserve the use of medication for situations in which this approach may fail. This is not to suggest, however, that you will hardly ever need to resort to medication. In fact, combination of low doses of medication plus the nondrug strategies may provide the best mix for many patients.

One ought not to maintain a fixed allegiance to drugs as the solution for every problem, nor a fixed aversion to them either. As the child of a demented parent, you need to exercise judgment as to what is best for your mom or dad. In the discussion of these problems of psychic suffering, your decision making must constantly recall one of the "laws" of dementia:

> *All emotions are as equally powerful in dementia as in normal life—it is not how things really are, but how we think they are, that governs our emotions.*

What does it mean for the emotional "feel" to remain the same for a demented person as for a normal person? The implication is that imaginary burglars are just as terrifying for your parent as a real burglar would be for you! Wandering lost in the neighborhood for your parent is as fearful as wandering lost in the woods would be for you. Anger, suspicion, rage, agitation, fear—all are forms of psychic pain and suffering that feel the same for your parent as they feel to you. Such psychic suffering should never be accepted without an attempt at alleviation. Words and gestures may help; emotional support may help; but when medication is needed, it should not be withheld.

Before resorting to medication, you would be well advised to try to restructure you parent's living patterns. Much of the unpleasant behaviors of a demented individual are the same behaviors of which everyone is capable—pacing, cursing, hitting, and screaming. The significant difference is the degree of provocation. Whereas it might take extraordinary circumstances to push a normal person to such loss of control, a demented person's identical actions appear inappropriate because the general public does not recognize how much easier it is to overwhelm the nervous system of a person with dementia.

Before resorting to medication, therefore, try the following:

- Attempt to identify positive, pleasant events in your parent's daily life. Do not make value judgments! Do not assume that simple, boring, monotonous activities could not possibly be pleasurable to any adult. Very often these are precisely the types of overlooked activities that are most pleasing to a person with dementia.
- Start with a few, but then try to maximize the number of similar pleasant events each day.
- At the same time, observe for negative experiences and, wherever possible, minimize them.
- Simplify the environment, removing all unnecessary objects except those that have a positive emotional or sentimental value; do not allow decorative clutter, which tends to overwhelm a person with dementia.
- Teach caregivers to try to distract your parent if agitation and upset develop, rather than try to argue with them.

For the most part, the medications used to ease these expressions of psychic suffering do not actually improve your parent's understanding. Rather, medication acts by defusing the emotional component of whatever is leading to repetition, agitation, tantrums, or hallucination. As a general rule, tranquilizers are most effective if used in a manner so as to minimize any unwanted impact of the drug on alertness and balance. For each of the problems discussed, tranquilizer medication may be necessary, and should be used according to the following guidelines:

- Start at the lowest dose that the manufacturer makes. If your parent is historically sensitive to drugs, ask for a medication that comes in liquid or concentrate. Not only may this be easier to swallow (or disguise), but it will allow you to use just a few drops to achieve doses much smaller than those provided by the drug company for the "average" adult.

- Realize that it takes less medicine to defuse an emotion before it occurs than to suppress an emotion once it is present. If your parent suffers only the occasional outburst, it may be fine to keep the pills in the bottle and use them only as necessary. Still, if emotional upset does occur and if nondrug strategies are not working, you will find no advantage in a lengthy delay that will result in large doses to control a growing agitation or rage. Similarly, if experience has shown that certain problems are appearing on a regular basis, give a low dose of the drug in anticipation of the problem.

A typically predictable situation is that of "sundowning." Sundowning is the appearance of confusion or hallucination in the early evening, sometimes in an elderly person who appears perfectly fine during the day. The term accurately suggests that the problems tend to occur when the sun goes down, although no one has yet devised a scientifically acceptable theory as to why this should be. Nevertheless, experience suggests that it is better to give a low dose of medication at four o'clock to prevent hallucination than to resort to higher doses at eight o'clock, when the hallucinations have stirred up anxiety and confusion.

- Choose your medication by side effect! Sometimes a drug's "side effects" can be turned to advantage, but in all cases you should consider how well positioned your parent is to cope with the effects of each drug. If your parent also has high blood pressure, for example, a drug like Thorazine that tends to lower blood pressure may allow your doctor to reduce the dose of your parent's blood pressure medication. Constipation from a drug may be beneficial if your parent tends to have loose bowel movements, but even if this is not true, you may be able to easily cope with such a side effect by simply adding more bran cereal. On the other hand, a drug like Haldol may lead to some stiffening of muscles and slowing of movement. If your parent's balance and walking are already very unsteady, this is probably a drug to avoid if possible.

- Even if you have found a medication and a routine that works (e.g., 0.5 milligrams of Haldol every morning, with another late-afternoon dose to head off sundowning), you should consider trying to cut back or eliminate the medication every six to twelve months. Dementia and aging are both dynamic processes; giving your 79-year-old mother 1 milligram of Haldol will not be the same as giving your 80-year-old mother 1 milligram of Haldol next year. Dementia changes the brain, and time changes the liver and kidneys too, so that 1 milligram of drug next year may be too potent for her. Alternatively, the emotional outbursts that are present this year may or may not exist next year as your parent's dementia progresses.

Tranquilizers cannot make memory better, nor can they eliminate confusion. But they can uncouple a confused idea from the "logical" emotional consequences. They create indifference to the "strange man" in the bedroom, to the "unfamiliar" room, to the imaginary "children running through the house." Such indifference can stabilize a demented parent in their own home, allowing you and home care workers to care for your parent with greater effectiveness. And most importantly, the peace of mind a well-chosen medication may bring to your mom or dad is no less valuable for being artificial.

— 7

Repetition

IT IS OUR MEMORY for the past that consoles us for the present. Living with short-term memory loss means living in a world cut off from that reassurance. For example, you may feel secure that your child is well if you spoke with him or her this morning. But what if no word had been heard for days or weeks? Would you not be, understandably, anxious? Likewise, your parent's anxiety is equally understandable. With short-term memory loss, the abstract concept of "this morning" has no existence and therefore no power to reassure. The last recalled long-term memory may be weeks or months old. From this troubling and painful fact comes the constant repetitive questioning, often as frequently as every few minutes.

Being repeatedly asked the same question by your demented parent can drive you mad. Many children feel reluctant to admit they feel this way, as if becoming inpatient with a sick mom or dad is cause for shame. In fact, everyone's sanity can be sorely tested by parental repetitiveness. Breaking the cycle is important to you and your parent as well. The anxiety that underlies the constant questioning is more a source of psychic pain to your mother or father than it is to you.

To break the cycle, you need to enter imaginatively into

your parent's world and identify the anxiety behind the question. You must discover what the question *means* to your parent on an emotional level. The emotional meaning is related, but is rarely identical, to the actual content of the question being asked. Once this emotional meaning has been identified, you will be in a position to execute an act of preemptive reassurance. For example, in the case of repeated telephone inquiries, you may guess the source of the anxiety and place next to your parent's telephone a note that states in block letters, Everybody Is Fine, I Will Call You in the Morning.

It is not information itself that is being sought but rather reassurance. In personal conversation, you may be better able to defuse repetition with a good guess as to the latent anxiety behind the question than with endless answers. In general, any answer that covers the basic sources of human anxiety—that everything and everybody is well, and that you will always be there to care for them—will be more meaningful than expecting your parent to provide their own internal translation from a factual answer into self-reassurance.

In ordinary, everyday life, most people are not accustomed to giving emotionally powerful responses to mundane questions:

Q: Where is your brother? Shouldn't he be here?
A: You know I love you and will stay here and take care of you.

This is a skill to be learned if you and your parent are to share some semblance of mental peace. But even if you cannot find the right words to penetrate the core of your parent's anxieties, you still have several fallback strategies:

1. Change the subject or distract the person with an entirely different conversation or simple task. You can often reasonably hope that if you can keep the question out of mind for longer than its usual repeat cycle (measured often in minutes), it will disappear on its own.

2. Ignore the question. This sometimes works, although it can also backfire into a crescendo of agitation and emotional upset that proves more upsetting than the repetition (especially in a public place).

3. Use a tranquilizer. It may not be the first choice, but neither is it a choice to be avoided at all costs. It is far better to accept a low dose of a medication to ease anxiety than to pursue an ideology of avoiding medication. Although this decision will need to be ratified by your doctor who will prescribe the medication, you may have better results if you suggest a low dose of one of the following:

- Haldol
- Ativan
- Buspar
- Cognex

Among these, only Cognex may actually improve memory slightly, enough to break the cycle of repetition by keeping both answer and question better retained in memory. The other drugs and their relatives make no claim to improving a person's memory but rather are targeted your parent's anxiety level—to slightly defuse the emotional drive for reassurance.

Ultimately, as the dementia process progresses into its middle stage, the problem of repetitiveness will disappear, in large part because the progression of neurological damage will reduce your parent's ability to use language to express anxiety. Be warned, however, that the inability to use words to voice anxiety may make *your* life easier, but it does not mean that the anxiety itself has disappeared! It is more likely that the anxiety will find expression in other, nonverbal expressions.

— 8

Nervous Confusion

WITH THE PROGRESSION OF DEMENTIA, there may develop states of agitation that display themselves in confused, disoriented behavior rather than in persistent questioning. At this stage, "retrograde amnesia" is generally well established and a principal contributor to the problem. Retrograde amnesia is the loss of memory starting with the most recent, short-term memories in a person's life, that loss gradually extending ever further back into their past. This amnesia may begin to create problems as the demented parent's memory point of reference recedes back too many years into a vanished past. The "president" may be Franklin Roosevelt; dead relatives may be remembered still young and alive, living in houses long since bulldozed out of existence.

Common problematic scenarios created by retrograde amnesia include the following:

Nonrecognition of One's Spouse: The demented person's spouse will not be recognized, the memory of "husband" or "wife" now existing mentally only as that person looked twenty or thirty years ago. Your demented mother's agitation may never be understood, therefore, until you look at your father through her eyes and see a strange man walking in her house and sleeping in her bed. Burglar? Rapist? Is she not the only sane one present—is her agitation not the only logical response to such a situation? Is there not something very odd about *your* behavior, to act as if nothing is wrong?

Concern for the Children: Retrograde amnesia may have erased the memory of adult children; "you" may exist when you are present before your parent's field of vision, but five minutes after you depart, the only recollection of a son or daughter may be of a young, school-aged child. Late afternoon agitation may be the expression of a mother's need to be home when "you" come home from school. Who will let you in? What will happen to you? Although this particular schoolday concern is almost exclusively found in women, both men and women share a common experience of anxiety about the whereabouts or safety of their children.

Concern for the Job: Because of the social history of most of this century, this is almost always a source of male agitation (curiously, even in women who worked much of their adult lives). Typically this may be the source of agitation in the self-employed businessman, where a lifetime's sense of personal responsibility survives longer than the recollection of retirement.

Unfamiliar Surroundings: The recognition of one's present home may be lost throught the process of retrograde amnesia. The shorter the time mom or dad has lived in their present dwelling, the more vulnerable they are to being ill at ease in their own home. This is a particular source for extreme agitation when "home" is transferred to a nursing home, but even the memory of a home that has been lived in for the past ten or twenty years may be erased after a few years of retrograde amnesia. Once the recognition of being safe at home is lost, your parent's "logical" assessment of the situation can create very serious degrees of agitation, possibly including a plan to escape this unfamiliar place and head to the "home" of yesteryear. Why am I here? How did I get here? If I don't know where I am, neither does my family.

They must be worried! All of these logical conclusions, perhaps not verbalized to you, may stir your mom or dad into a state of anxiety from which confused and possibly dangerous behavior may result.

Worry About Money: The idea that money is necessary to survive in life seems to persist fairly well, but the recollection of where the bank accounts are and how much money is (or is not) in those accounts is a powerful source of continued anxiety and agitation. Never think that your demented parent is not psychologically "aware" of money simply because you are paying the bills. It may be precisely the absence of any reassuring possession of a checkbook or bank book that drives a demented person's agitation!

Worry About Parents: In a most ironic twist, retrograde amnesia will often erase the memory of the death of your grandparents, leaving your own parent with the mental picture of a living mother or father needing care. Where are they? Are they well?

Object Identification Problems: As part of the loss of abstraction with dementia comes a loss of language. Language is fundamentally an abstract exercise of the human mind, in which words or sounds are connected with a specific meaning. With early dementia, there are often memory lapses for the right word to finish a sentence. As dementia progresses, however, the destruction of language capability begins to strike at the very connection of word to object to meaning. A pillow on the bed may not be recognizable as a "pillow," but its shape may recall an animal; a wristwatch may be some bit of debris tightly stuck on that can't be easily dislodged. Repetitive touching of an object, picking it up and putting it down, in a state of agitation usually means that the object is being misidentified as a source of something upsetting.

Overall one might naively think that it would be pleasant to have retrograde amnesia, as if the dementia is providing its own anesthetic to the problems of today by taking its victims back to happier times. This is rarely the case. The usual result of retrograde amnesia is anxiety. If that anxiety can no longer be expressed in verbal language, it will still be expressed, diffusing through your parent's entire conscious being. It is precisely because the human mind—even when wounded by dementia—never ceases its efforts to make rational sense out of the world. This inherent part of being human does not end until consciousness itself no longer exists.

One ought not to hold an unreasonable prejudice against medications, but many doctors are too quick to rely upon drugs to control agitated confusion. They resort to this reflexive response because they cannot imagine that such a demonstrably confused person is, in fact, thinking in a perfectly logical and rational way. A confused demented person is actually making perfectly logical use of seriously incorrect information and will continue to struggle to do so as long as possible. Responding with ever higher doses of medication to "suppress" the confusion may lead to sedation verging on unconsciousness.

Realizing that confusion in dementia is the result of applying correct logic to an incorrect premise opens the possiblity that you may be able to accomplish more than the doctor can by combining your superior knowledge of your parent's personal history with a little bit of immagination. It is always worth the effort to try to imaginatively enter into your parent's frame of reference. Cut yourself off temporarily from the "reality" of the present, and from your parent's confused words try to reconstruct the time and place from which your parent is operating at the moment.

Despite the glib phrase "second childhood," retrograde amnesia rarely seems to deposit demented persons back into young childhood. The most common scenario is that of young middle age. With this as a starting point, try to listen again to what your mother or father is saying. What frame of reference is he or she operating in? If you can make the imaginative leap, you will discover to your surprise that within this new frame of reference, the words of your mother or father now make perfect sense. Thereafter try to talk and offer your reassurance within the context of the time and place being occupied in their demented mind. You will be much more successful in defusing anxiety by surrendering yourself temporarily to a delusional world than you will be if you insist upon trying to correct your parent's "error" and reorienting your mom or dad to the reality of *your* time and place. If you insist upon the latter, you will almost surely fail. At worst you will exacerbate the situation.

Remember that the goal is to reassure and calm your mother or father. The goal is *not* to correct erroneous thinking, not to win the argument, and not, necessarily, to tell the truth.

Do not fear that you will perpetuate their deluded sense of time and place by giving in to their disoriented conviction of time and place. This fear seems to be instinctive among family members of demented individuals. They tend to believe that yielding to delusional thinking will leave their mother or father more helplessly lost in the past. Many children feel they are obligated to struggle constantly with the process of endless reorientation to the present.

This approach is fine if your parent's dementia is mild and the confusion is limited to low-anxiety issues and questions like "What day is today?" Once moderate dementia is present, however, an unyielding strategy of reorientation may backfire. If, for example, your father indicates he is worried about his own mother, reorienting him to the fact that his mother died years ago may trigger a shoking emotional upset as "real" as if the news of his mother's death were being broken to him for the first time! Often such attempts at correcting other "errors" may lead not to reorientation but rather to arguments or suspicion about your motives in lying.

You will not, as many believe, reinforce error if you don't correct it. Your best options are similar to those discussed in relation to repetitiveness:

Preempt agitation whenever possible: If written words still are intelligible at your parent's level of dementia, try leaving written notes that convey the basics of reassurance. Some examples might be This Is Your Home. You Are Safe Here or I Will Be Coming to See You After Work or perhaps The Children Are Being Taken Care Of.

Clocks, calendars, written notes, or labels may assist you. As language fades, it may be sufficient to distribute some enlarged photographs of your face, smiling, where they can be seen as a source of non-verbal reassurance that you still exist.

Accept the error and offer reassurance: If telling them that a deceased family member is well gives pleasure and reassurance, do so! Give your father a dummy bankbook with large figures typed in or a dummy checkbook. Neither forgery will need to be first-rate to be accepted. Devise any serviceable lie, and do not fear that you will perpetuate error. More than likely, your reassurance will allow your parent to let go of the idea, and it may pass thus into the abyss of short-term memory loss.

Change the subject: Even if you cannot guess the source of your parent's anxiety, you may be able to redirect attention to another topic. You may only need to sustain this new activity for a few minutes while you hope for the "logical" train of thought that is perpetuating the anxiety to disappear into short-term memory loss.

Simplify the environment: If you notice that your mother or father seems to become upset while repetitively touching or walking over to an object, try to remove it. You may never be able to fathom how the object is being misidentified by your mom's or dad's confused mind, but it is common for the meanings of physical objects to become distorted by dementia. A woolen cap may be perceived as a frightening small animal, or a coat on a hanger may appear to be a man hiding in the closet. If your parent seems predisposed to this trait, it may be best to light the room well to optimize the opportunity for correct identification of objects. Even so, try to keep the room bare of all but the most essential objects. Both strategies will reduce the chance for perceptual errors as a cause for agitation.

Medication: Medication is particularly valuable when agitated confusion persists despite your best attempts. It is often essential in those situations where you cannot provide a familiar and reassuring environment. Travel outside is sometimes pleasing to a demented person if it occurs in the presence of well-known and trusted individuals, but this is not always the case and not always possible. Some tranquilizer medication may be essential for a trip to the doctor's office; a change of home care workers may precipitate a degree of emotional upset that will respond to nothing else.

Not all cases of agitated confusion can be easily managed. In many cases, some agitation appears to be inescapable—as if so many aspects of life are confusing and threatening that no handful of strategies suffice. In these situations, the use of medication is the only compassionate strategy to follow. Realize, however, that dementia is a progressive disorder, and that as it progresses there may come a time when much of the mental raw material that feeds your parent's agitated confusion may have vanished. Even the successful use of medication for agitated confusion ought to be stopped on at least an annual basis, to see if the need for it still continues.

— 9 —

Getting Lost

NOT EVERY DEMENTED PERSON WANDERS. The majority of persons with dementia, in fact, are naturally intimidated by the noise and confusion of the world outside their home and adopt such a strong affinity for the place they know that the more common problem is convincing the parent to leave, even in their child's company.

Nevertheless, some demented persons do walk outside unsupervised and with only the most vague and often erroneous idea of where they are going or how they will return. Wandering is one of the most dreaded of problems derived from retrograde amnesia in the moderately demented parent. Each winter brings another story in the local paper of a demented man or woman who died of exposure after wandering out of their home. Were it not for the voluntary attentiveness of neighbors and doormen, the number would likely be increased twentyfold.

Wandering tends to represent a more visceral degree of agitation. With simpler expressions of agitation, you can usually find some success with nondrug strategies or the use of tranquilizer drugs if you fail to identify the operative frame of reference which is creating the anxiety. Wandering, however, is different. A confused parent whose memory reference point makes "home" unrecognizable, and who is driven to leave this strange place, will not be easily dissuaded by a gentle dose of tranquilizer. There is in fact *no* medication that will stop this behavior, short of a dose so strong that your parent can't stand up and get to the door. Ironically, some major tranquilizers can over time induce a feeling of "restless leg syndrome" that may even make wandering worse! Overall, the control of this serious problem requires a variety of strategies, implemented together.

Suggested strategies include as much of the following as you can do:

- First, assume that whatever you do will fail, and that your parent will get out onto the street alone. Enroll your parent in "Safe Return," the program run by the Alzheimer's Association (your parent does not have to have proven Alzheimer's disease to qualify, only dementia). For a cost of about twenty dollars, your mom or dad will be enrolled in a national database, as well as be provided with an ID bracelet, necklace, clothing tags, and identification card. Place an identification card in your parent's wallet or purse with your parent's name, address, and *your* phone number. Add redundancy to this fail-safe plan by also having your parent wear a wrist or ankle ID bracelet with the same information. Alert every trustworthy neighbor, storeowner, and, if your parent lives in an apartment, the doorman. Let each know that the sight of your parent out alone is a sign that something is wrong, even if he or she appears well.

- Place a sign on the door that says in simple printed letters Don't Go Out. You may add You Are in Your Own Home for some additional reality orientation, or use some other personalized deterrent such as John Will Meet You Here. Curiously, you may also wish to label the door to the bathroom with a sign or drawing of a toilet, there being cases of a demented person leaving their apartment not intending to wander but rather to look for the bathroom and then becoming disoriented once outside!

- Purchase a clock that provides digital A.M. and P.M. readouts, preferably with a day/night face, and leave it next to your parent's bed. Not uncommonly, a parent will awaken at 3:00 A.M. and misinterpret the time to be 3:00 P.M. and leave in the middle of the night. Even with twenty-four hour home care, a sleeping home attendant may not realize that your parent is missing. Added insurance may come from simple bells or sound alarms on the doors.

- Investigate the use of safety locks or doorknob covers that offer some deterrence against exit. There is a fine line in terms of fire safety, and some other person should be available in the event of an emergency.

- Imaginative strategies include leaving a home video cassette playing on the television. The familiar faces and voices may suffice to keep your parent comfortably placed in a chair for few hours even in your absence. Because of short-term memory loss, replaying the same tape twice a day, every day, is unlikely to ever become boring or stale.

- Wandering alone is reason to consider a home care worker for eight or twelve hours a day. Alternatively, if an Alzheimer's disease day-care center is available, and if travel outside the home appears to be a strong urge in your parent, you may obtain more peace of mind by signing up to have your parent transported to the center for the day.

- Keep on hand a recent photo, as well as an unlaundered item of clothing in a zip-locked plastic bag. These somewhat macabre steps may someday prove lifesaving, allowing either human or canine searchers to find your parent before the effects of the elements take their often fatal toll.

- Try to disguise the appearance of the front door from the inside, perhaps with a painting to make it appear to be a part of the wall.

There is one last important safety issue related to wandering that deserves particular mention and consideration. Realize that not every fatality related to wandering comes from the outside world. Some demented persons will wander through the kitchen and, if unobserved, turn on the oven or stove before wandering off again, completely forgetting their action. Surprisingly, this occurs fairly infrequently given the large numbers of persons with dementia. The majority of demented individuals regard kitchen appliances with an attitude similar to their regard for the world outside their homes—as too complicated to deal with and best avoided. Yet for the demented person who feels at ease turning on the stove, there is very little in either medication or strategy that will afford safety. Even a home care worker whose only lapse in vigilance is the few moments it takes to use the bathroom can return to find a fire already out of control. If your parent ever touches the stove, even to place a teakettle on an unlit burner, have your electrician or the gas company devise a hidden cutoff switch to ensure that the stove is never accessible to your mother or father.

10

Imagining Things

ONE OF THE MOST CURIOUS and inexplicable qualities of dementia is the tendency for the dementia-injured brain to create visual scenes whose origin is entirely in the brain itself. These "visions" are called hallucinations. Hallucinations are a close cousin of delusions, which are the visual misinterpretation of an object that does in fact exist. Seeing a sock on the floor as a mouse is a delusion; seeing an imaginary dog in the living room is a hallucination.

Demented persons have a fair frequency of hallucination, although the numbers reported suggest that it is a problem that afflicts only a minority of individuals. The curious nature of hallucination does not rest only on the fact that it occurs but also on the fact that despite the differences in people's lives, there is a restricted number of visions that occur. Typically, a demented person will see one or more children, usually running through the house, dogs running under the bed, or a strange man who may be in the living room, in the bedroom, or at the window.

Why these visions and not others? Why dogs and never cats? Why running children? Why will the man be at the window but not the door; the living room but not the bathroom? In some ways, the limited number of repeated themes of dementia hallucination is more intriguing than the existence of hallucination itself. So predictable are these subject choices of the demented mind that the report of other more colorful or elaborate hallucinations should be reported to your doctor. Some drugs, especially drugs for Parkinson's disease, will generate much more detailed and exotic visions, such as an English countryside with sheep and shepherds viewed through a city apartment window!

Some demented persons will begin their hallucination early in the day, but for the average person it is unusual for hallucinations to be generated until the late afternoon or early evening. The predictability of this time of day has been noted by families for decades and has given rise to the term "sundowning." Typically, with sundowning, a person functioning fairly well during the daytime will give an appearance of increased anxiety and confusion each afternoon, followed by the appearance of the hallucination by evening time. This pattern may persist for weeks or months.

Scientific debate continues on why the setting sun should be connected with rising mental dysfunction. Some think it is only coincidental—that the real issue is fatigue by the end of the day that causes the mind to malfunction. According to this argument, an elderly person who has been up all day naturally would be most fatigued by evening, accounting for the appearance of the hallucination at that time of the day.

Others believe a connection exists between the disappearance of sunlight and the appearance of the hallucination—either that the gathering darkness casts shadows that confound the mind and invite hallucination or that the removal of sunlight itself causes a chemical change in the brain. In fact, no one knows for certain the cause of hallucinations or the reason they tend to appear, and turning on the lights indoors does not mean that the vivid visual images of deceased relations, small animals, children, or burglars will evaporate.

What is to be done about hallucination? There are several points to keep in mind:

- In the first place, not every hallucination needs to be eradicated. Some demented persons hallucinate only on the rare occasion, and some who hallucinate are not always troubled by it. Rarely do they actually enjoy the experience, but it is not uncommon to find that they may be aware of the unreality of their hallucination even while it is occurring. They will tell you that they do in fact see a dog but logically know a dog cannot be in their room. If your parent is not emotionally distressed by the hallucination you may choose to talk about it as an "experience."

- Remember that hallucinations are *real*, even if they are an imaginary reality! It rarely helps to contradict your hallucinating parent, since your words alone will not cause their brains to function differently. You may be honest and tell your parent that *you* do not see a dog in the room, but you invite agitation (and would also be incorrect) if you tried to argue that *your parent* is not seeing a dog. Insofar as we all "see" with our minds, philosophically the dog that your brain does not see has no greater claim to truth than the dog your parent's brain does see!

  If you are present during your parent's hallucinatory experience, therefore, do not argue. You may try to dispel the hallucination by turning on the lights (which sometimes helps, but not always) and remaining in the room with your mother or father (the presence of a real human being will often dispel the imaginary one). And, to be philosophically correct, you may be honest in stating what it is you don't see, so long as you do not dispute the reality of your parent's experience.

- You may try to take advantage of the limited repertoire of the typical hallucination by moving your parent from one of the rooms where hallucinations tend to occur (living room or bedroom) into another part of the house. Rarely does the hallucination follow, and once banished, it may not return again that night.

- Ultimately, the control of hallucinations requires a special class of medication, called antipsychotics. There are about a dozen of these, and the most helpful are listed and discussed at the end of this book. One important difference among these drugs is the extent to which they sedate the patient. For late-afternoon hallucination, you may prefer one of the less sedating drugs, so as not to interfere with dinner. At night one of the most effective is Mellaril (thioridazine), whose sedating quality is a detriment during the day but which may help reinforce sleep if used at night.

Some sons and daughters refuse to use tranquilizers on general principles. This intent is always laudable, so long as it is your parent's welfare and not ideology that is the prime concern. Sadly, however, some offspring allow their mother or father to suffer a great deal of unnecessary psychic pain because they don't "believe" in drugs or because the little child in them selfishly wants the parent to still look like the mom or dad they knew. Even if you are willing to live with your parent's confusion, agitation, and hallucination, it is not right to let them suffer as well.

11

Emotional Outbursts

THERE MAY COME A POINT when a mother or father reknowned throughout life for a gentle and calm demeanor becomes prone to outbursts of hostility, anger, and perhaps outright belligerence, with hitting or scratching. Such tantrums do more than shock family members unaccustomed to seeing mom or dad behave so out of character. Episodes of hostile or aggresive behavior may cause a home care worker to quit, sometimes with little notice and not uncommonly at the worst possible time.

Hostile outbursts generally develop when several factors come together in the life of a demented person. The first requirement is for at least a moderately severe degree of mental detioration to have been reached, such that your mother or father may be subject to the temporary loss of recognition of people and places. The second requirment is that language has usually been heavily affected, such that it is difficult for your parent to express feelings in words. When the third element of sensory overload is added to the situation, there will be a high risk for the occurrence of tantrum behavior, with screaming, intransigence, and belligerence. A calm and docile father can suddenly be fighting and screaming; a mother who was as gentle as a lamb while watching TV may start clawing and scratching the home care worker's hands at bath time.

There is a sad tendency for families faced with such swings in behavior to read incorrect meanings into them. Families may erroneously conclude that the demented person is looking for attention in such behavior or is seeking to manipulate the situation. They are wrong. The demented person is neither a two-year-old child nor an adult who has become spoiled or willful. These emotional outbursts are not the calculated expressions of a scheming mind but rather the product of a weakened mind overloaded to the point of emotional breakdown.

Demented persons are always mentally working with either incomplete or erroneous information being fed to them by their damaged memory systems. Moment to moment, they are always straining their hardest to make the best and most logical use of the information available to them. Emotional outbursts will occur when there is a catastrophic failure of this ability to make sense of the world—the people, the voices, the instructions, and the noise.

One factor in precipitating emotional outbursts, therefore, is fatigue. It is true of dementia as it is of all neurological diseases that the deficits of the disease will always be greater when a person is tired. This is true of the young woman with multiple sclerosis and of the patient with Parkinson's disease; it is also true of the demented patient. A tired person with dementia will be at an additional disadvantage in trying to follow what is going on and in finding psychological comfort in whatever sense can be made of the world.

While fatigue may set up a demented person for an emotional outburst, the actual onset of tantrum behavior generally follows when there is some additional sensory overload. It is difficult for a normal person to imagine how little stimulation can be too much for a demented person to cope with. A trip to the restaurant, for example, can be deceptively simple from the perspective of a normal, healthy adult. The demented person's role may appear to be simple, since all of the details and decisions appear to have been made by others; seemingly, your parent's role is confined to enjoying the trip. In reality, the emotional stress is much greater for your mom or dad, who from moment to moment needs to strain mentally to reconcile new faces, new rooms, traffic, noise, direction, destination, and so on—while all the time struggling to remember the purpose of it all!

In fact, many minor activities of daily living consist of a large number of steps, in sequence, leading to one purpose. A normal person tends to lump all of these sequences into one "action," like taking a bath, going for a walk, and getting undressed for bed. To a demented person, each button, zipper, and sleeve is a new task, whose purpose is not at all clear or obvious and whose execution is far from trivial. Stringing these actions together may suddenly appear overwhelming and confusing. The reaction comes in an outpouring of emotionally charged resistance to being ordered about or touched.

Willful resistance can be often be handled by a change in tactics. In the first place, you must recognize that these emotional explosions are most likely to occur when your parent is too tired and the events and expectations surrounding him or her are one or more of the following:

• too new
• too much
• too fast

When faced with such a behavioral and emotional crisis, the following actions should be put into effect at once:

• The first step is to back off. Stop whatever activity is in progress, since it evidently overwhelms your parent's limited ability to cope.
• Next, approach in a slow and gentle manner. Do not let your voice reflect the anger, rage, or upset that is being demonstrated by your parent. Even if the content of your words is not being readily understood, the soft and soothing tone of your voice will communicate nonverbally with the emotional centers of the brain. These

emotional centers of the brain are more "primitive" than the language centers and, because of their relative simplicity, are actually more resistant to damage by the process of dementia. You may be able to get your message through to these emotional centers better by the sound of your voice than by the language content of your words, a content which may be garbled by dementia damage to language centers.

- Touch is another important nonverbal communication tool that can help defuse an emotional outburst and is much better than talk. More talk can add to the burden of sensory information that needs to be decoded and interpreted. More talk can be like throwing fuel onto the fire. Touch, however, can convey feelings that do not need complex interpretation in order to be understood. Try to soothingly rub and caress, with hugs and kisses. Such gestures will defuse the mental perception of threat.

  The aging process tends to reduce tactile sensitivity of an older person's hands, while leaving touch sensation intact closer to the trunk. Try to maximize your reassuring touch at the upper arms, or give a gentle hug about the shoulders.

- Seek to convey that all is well, and that together you and your parent will simply do one step at a time. When you do talk to your mom or dad during this crisis, do so in a calm, steady voice. If verbal commands are not being followed—for example, to lift one foot onto a step—use your hands to guide the limb into the movement you want. Demented persons will generally follow tactile guidance better than they will verbal instructions, again since directions indicated by touch do not seem to need the sophisticated mental processing and translation that verbal directions require.

Equally important in the management of this behavior are the things experience suggests you ought not to do. In particular:

- Do not try to argue with your parent nor to scold or command them. Shrill orders will only heighten their sensory overload.
- It is best not to attempt brute physical force. Even frail persons, in a state of rage, can be surprisingly strong.
- Don't allow a circle of well-meaning helpers to form about you. More people with more faces will add to the sensory overload.

And, of course, don't keep making the same mistake over and over! If certain activities tend to strain your parent to the breaking point, try either to eliminate them or to reschedule them for a better part of the day. As a rule, any scheduled outings, walks, visits, or doctor appointments should be made in the morning. Fatigue generally makes the late afternoon more problematic for demented people.

Of course, there may be days when soothing talk and gentle persuasion alone do not suffice for a key issue. Typically this is an isolated refusal in an otherwise manageable individual, who may, for example, absolutely refuse to take medication or a bath but otherwise shows a high degree of cooperability. If behavioral resistance is very narrowly focused on just one issue, you may need to invest a bit more imaginative thought into the process. There may be some fixed idea that your mother or father cannot relinquish. Common issues are refusal to undress in front of strangers, especially if of the opposite sex, or a paranoid idea that the medication is poison. If imaginative solutions cannot be found, you may ultimately need to resort to medication.

— 12 —————————————————

Distrust and Suspicion

PARANOIA HAS SEVERAL FACES in dementia. Most commonly, paranoia is the "logical" conclusion of a demented mind faced with a series of disappearances and lost objects that cannot reasonably be attributed to coincidence. Too much is missing to be explained in any way other than by theft, and if there is a thief, then who is it? Suspicion naturally falls upon home care workers, who bear the brunt of accusations for the theft of money, pocketbooks, combs, hairpins, and every other object that has been put down someplace and forgotten. Of course, sometimes it is true that the home care worker may also be a thief, but if so, there ought to be some clear evidence beyond your parent's charges. Experience suggests that such occurrences are very rare, and it is easy to name scores of devoted home care workers for every one who might have been dishonest.

Complaints of physical abuse by demented persons may also be merely a paranoid interpretation of the worker's insistence upon bathing or washing, but such charges by a demented person are statistically much less common than charges of stealing food or money and should not be dismissed out of hand. Home care workers have been known to be abusive, particularly with demented persons who are prone to annoying degrees of repetition or frequent tantrum behavior. Honesty and patience are two different virtues. A home care worker may have neither the temptation nor the desire to steal any of your parent's household items but may be short on patience in the face of behavior that is very difficult for anybody to manage every day.

Again, one would like to have evidence of that abuse, although there are times when you must just listen to that indefinable inner voice that tells you it's time to change home care workers. Be suspicious in this regard of black-and-blue marks. Old persons frequently get these on the hands and forearms from delicate skin, particularly if they take aspirin, but marks on the upper arms and body always mean trauma of some sort, either falling, stumbling, or possibly abuse.

Coping with paranoia is very difficult. It does not yield easily to behavioral manipulation. Arguing with your parent may well make them more upset; ignoring the paranoid suspicions or changing the subject does not work as easily as for repetitiveness or other forms of agitated behavior. Even in a brain whose memory function is riddled with deficits, the idea of thievery seems still able to find root and take hold. People who cannot consistently remember their children's names will still remember to glare suspiciously at the home care worker.

You may be able to defuse some paranoid charges by helping to find the "stolen" items where your parent left them, but generally the treatment for paranoid symptoms fall into one of two categories:

1. *Acceptance and indulgence*. There has long been a perception among some members of the higher socio-economic classes that "servants" are constitutionally prone to stealing. Some demented persons (who see their home care workers as maids or cleaning ladies anyway) may complain about "thievery" but do not indicate genuine fright or feel personally assaulted. These situations are probably best left alone. Indeed, at a time in life when there are very few superior qualities your parent still possesses, a sense of moral superiority may be a final bastion of self-respect.

2. *Drug treatment*. If paranoia is accompanied by fear and agitation, or if paranoid suspicions are causing resistance to taking medication or food (due to fear of poisoning), there is no real alternative to the use of tranquilizer drugs. If the paranoia has already escalated to the point where your parent is refusing to take medication, you may need to resort to once-monthly injections of long-acting tranquilizers or to liquid forms of these medications that can be disguised in food (particularly Haldol, which is not only very effective for paranoid delusions but also odorless and tasteless). It may seem a bit disreputable, but it is effective.

Of course, your victory in most of the struggles described in this chapter could be easily ensured by the regular use of tranquilizer medication. Such easily purchased victory may not be worth the price: Regular use of medication causes a reduction in the "personhood" of your parent. The remaining sparks of personality will be dimmer; whatever spontaneity of talk and action is left will be lessened; and proportionate with the dose will come an erosion of steadiness and balance. There is no way to predict exactly how your parent will react to a particular medication. Some demented persons pay a big price in side effects at fairly low doses; others can take larger doses with good benefit which far outweighs any detriment. But whether great or small, every demented person will pay some price for the use of medication.

Nevertheless, as the child of a demented parent, it will be your role to exercise your judgment as to what is best for your parent, and when medication is the correct recourse, in lieu of leaving your parent twisting helplessly in emotional winds beyond their self-control. Remember that with hallucination, paranoia, emotional outbursts, and belligerence, *the fact that the emotional experience has no apparent basis in "fact" does not in any way dilute the force of the experience for your parent!* Each and every one of these experiences is as unpleasant for your parent as it is for you in the context of the "real" world (although mercifully, your parent's short-term memory loss may allow them to forget the episode sooner than you would). Emotional outbursts, belligerence, and hostile gestures that threaten your other parent or caregivers needs to be controlled! If low-dose daily tranquilizer medication is needed to do that, then whatever diminution of spirit and personality it extracts will need to be accepted. Merely seek to ensure that everyone involved understands that your parent is a person, not a "problem." Always remember with tranquilizer medication:

- Seek to use the lowest dose initially and increase it on an as-needed basis only, thereby always being sure that you will be using the lowest effective dose.
- Consider that it takes less drug to head off predictable problems than it does to suppress fully developed ones. Note if your parent's problems are daily or episodic; allow daily medication only for daily problems.
- Remember that all tranquilizers tend to work well about the same percentage of time. Choose your medication by side effect. Choose which side effects of a drug your parent can most easily live with, or which side effects might in fact be beneficial for other problems they are having.
- And finally, no matter how successful the medication, remember to give a one-week "drug holiday" at least once a year. Dementia is a dynamic disease, and its "problems" sometimes get better as the disease gets worse. Very poor memory may ease the confusion that poor memory struggled with. The time may come when today's torments too have faded from memory.

— 13 —————————————————————

Sleep Disturbances

THERE IS A TENDENCY for patients with dementia to reverse their sleep-wake cycles. This puts a tremendous strain on everyone around them. If your parent is living with you, problems with their sleep are very likely to put you into a state of sleep deprivation, with its associated irritability, fatigue, and risk of accidents. If your parent lives with a twenty-four-hour home care worker, the problem of sleep disturbance is one of the symptoms most likely to cause that person to quit—perhaps suddenly. Even if your parent lives alone, sleep disturbance may cause problems involving neighbors and co-op boards.

Some sleep disturbance is fairly benign and best accepted without a struggle. People with neurological disabilities of any type and of any age tend to tire more easily over the course of a day. If you parent goes to bed at 7 P.M., it is not reasonable to expect twelve hours of sleep to follow. If "sleep disturbance" simply means awakening to go to the bathroom, followed by a return to sleep, you might do better to accept that this is *not* a sleep disturbance and should *not* be treated.

One common "sleep disturbance" that ought to be ignored is the self-reporting by your parent of poor sleep. Unless you possess independent confirmation that your parent "didn't sleep a wink," you should do nothing more than offer a sympathetic ear. Elderly persons frequently report their sleep as being very poor in quality due to a tendency with age for people to spend less time in the deep, satisfying stages of sleep. Healthy old people often report a poor night's sleep even when witnesses can attest that they have slept all night, because of multiple, brief arousals of consciousness within the act of sleep.

Were it not for the fact that patients with small-stroke disease or Alzheimer's disease can be exquisitely sensitive to medication (including nonprescription medication), you might try a sleeping pill. The attempt, however, is always a gamble. Your well-intentioned efforts could, indeed, help your parent get a good night's sleep—or might precipitate an episode of confusion, lethargy, or falling with long-lasting consequences. The approach to sleep disorders needs to focus as much as possible on nondrug intervention first, with drug therapy to be used cautiously and sparingly.

In dealing with sleep disorders, the following nondrug steps and interventions should first be taken:

- Stop all caffeine, including tea and soda as well as coffee. The amount of time that it takes to eliminate caffeine from the human body lengthens as people age. By the seventh or eighth decade of life, this elimination time may be as long as twelve or fifteen hours, meaning that the caffeine from a morning cup of coffee may still be disturbing sleep at bedtime. Switch to decaf.
- Look for medications that might disturb sleep. Many antidepressants will interrupt sleep, including Prozac. Some stimulants given to demented persons, like Ritalin and Dexedrine, will interfere with sleep, and so too will many medications for asthma. Diuretics (also known as "water pills") may disturb sleep by increasing the amount of nightly urination.

  It may not be wise to unilaterally stop medication without discussing the issue with a doctor, but don't be too timid either. Try to recall why the medication was given in the first place. Many medications have a tendency to be continued long past the point at which they remain useful.

- Try to regularize the sleep routine. This strategy actually works with people of all ages. It relies upon setting a fixed, regular hour for bedtime, to be preceded by a standard presleep routine. The more stereotyped these presleep rituals are, the more effective the entire sleep induction process. For example, first washing the face, then brushing the teeth (or the dentures), then taking the evening medication, then putting on pajamas, then taking a glass of warm milk (with an optional teaspoon of brandy), then going to bed—the routine must be started at the same time each night and done in the identical sequence. In a few days, the person will, like a Pavlovian dog, have been conditioned by the process to fall asleep as the final step.

- Search for ways in which your parent can be occupied during the day with activity that is appropriate to their level of dementia. Elderly persons with dementia tend to live sedentary lives that provide little physical challenge. Gentle exercise like walking, or even the stimulation of an Alzheimer's disease day-care center, may lead to a more easily achieved and more thorough sleep at night.

- Once your parent is in bed, try to discourage the sensory stimulation of the brain that comes from listening to music or watching television. Reading is seldom a problem, since the memory and language losses of moderate dementia usually cause most persons to stop reading fairly early in the disease. Listening, however, is passive. Many persons with dementia may still listen to music, or even watch TV though they are unable to hold the content of the program in mind. It is, however, a misconception that listening to music or watching TV will relax a person and make sleep come easier. These activities stimulate the brain into a higher level of wakefulness.

Initiating sleeping medication in most demented persons is a very serious step and fraught with the potential for disaster. You must not even think of any kind of nighttime sedation (including so called "safe" nonprescription sleeping pills) unless all of these steps have been tried and there remains a serious degree of nocturnal awakening associated with one of the following:

- hallucination
- agitation
- nocturnal wandering
- nocturnal cooking or smoking with risk of fire
- the threat of caregiver burnout

The risks of nocturnal sedation cannot be reliably predicted beforehand. If medication must be used, it is best to select the lowest dose available of the safest medicine possible—and then reduce it in half! It is also wise, if your parent lives alone, to try to stay for the first few nights when the use of a sleeping pill is being started. If any adverse reactions do occur, it well probably be in the first three days.

There are several types of adverse reactions to sleeping pills to anticipate:

Incontinence: Emotionally upsetting but the least serious consequence of a sedative may be that your parent will sleep through the urge to urinate. If your parent is not humiliated by the thought of wearing a diaper to bed, you may judge this to be a satisfactory trade-off for the advantages of better sleep at night.

Falling: More disturbing potential problems arise if the urge to void (which is a very strong neurological signal) awakens your parent anyway, despite the sleeping pill. In that situation, attempting to walk to the bathroom with the sleeping medication still drugging the brain invites a loss of balance and falling. If dementia has already affected your parent's balance and posture, you must assume that their risk of falling will be very high if sleeping medication is used and if urinating at night is part of their pattern. Possible solutions may be to use a bedside commode, incontinence diapers, or a sleeping medication that also reduces the urge to urinate (doxepin).

Catastrophic Reaction: Also known as a "paranoid break," this is one of the least common but most memorable reactions you may ever witness in any human being. It is a combination of inconsolable agitation, fear, and paranoia. Attempts to intervene with either soothing words or efforts to offer tranquilizer medication will often be met with hostility or even violence.

Ironically, the cause of such terrified agitation is often medication intended to calm and sedate. Unpredictably, sedative medication may reach the wrong target in the brain. Rather than numbing its intended targets—those brain areas causing anxiety and insomnia—the medication may unpredictably turn off the higher, rational centers of the brain that are trying to cope with the confusion and disorder of a life lived in dementia. The temporary loss of this residual rationality as a result of sedative medication may lead to several hours during which the deepest and most primitive centers of the brain are left in unrestrained control of your mother's or father's mind.

By these warnings I do not suggest that sedatives should *never* be used, but they must be given only for clear and compelling reasons. If medication must be used, it is helpful to ask yourself which of the two types of sleep disturbance is the real problem with your parent's sleep: sleep induction or nocturnal awakening.

Is the problem just falling asleep initially? Once asleep, does the person have a reasonably comfortable night, perhaps getting up once or twice but falling quickly back to sleep again? If so, your parent has a problem with *sleep induction*, and you want a medication that acts quickly and dissipates rapidly from the body. A longer-acting medication might dull the reflexes when your parent tries to get up at night (usually to go to the bathroom), leading to a fall. Additionally, a longer-acting medication might cause your parent to sleep through the need to urinate, leading to incontinence. *If only the initial part of sleep is a problematic, you want a drug that acts for only a very few hours*.

The best medication for sleep induction is *chloral hydrate*. Historically this is an old drug, and it is available via prescription as either a capsule or a liquid. The liquid form of the medicine is known by the time-honored moniker of "knockout drops" (the essential ingredient of a Mickey Finn). The attributed potency of this drug in detective stories, however, comes from giving it with alcohol; alone it is not quite as powerful and has several benefits:

- It doesn't interact much with other medications.
- It acts quickly and is eliminated by the body quickly.
- It is fairly gentle, with no side effects other than its tendency to make a person very quickly drowsy.
- It comes in a liquid, of course, and can be given to persons who have trouble swallowing.
- It is eliminated by the liver instead of the kidneys; generally drugs eliminated by the liver pose fewer potential side effects.

If falling asleep is not the problem, then the issue is awakening too often during the night. The most helpful question to ask yourself about nocturnal awakening is why your parent is getting up at night. The answer may suggest some more specific tactic other than sedation to keep your parent sleeping. The five most common causes of interrupted sleep are as follows:

1. *The need to go to the bathroom*. This is the most common cause of sleep disruption. Invariably the need is to urinate rather than to move the bowels. As dementia progresses, the ability of the deteriorating brain to control the urge to urinate deteriorates. The reasons are complex, but

basically a reversal of bladder control develops, undoing the achievements won as a toddler in toilet training.

In dementia, the urinating system begins again to resemble that of an infant or very small child. When urine has filled a child's bladder to capacity, the bladder automatically empties. It does this by reflex, with a force and suddenness that a baby's undeveloped brain cannot control. The average toddler requires approximately two years of brain maturation in order to possess sufficient "brain power" to control this automatic bladder reflex long enough to get to a bathroom. By full adulthood, of course, the brain has such firm control over the bladder that even the most forceful and painful contractions of an overfull bladder will not lead to a socially inappropriate release of urine.

As dementia weakens the brain, however, it also weakens the brain's control of the bladder. After decades of subservience, the bladder begins to reassert its independence. The brain of a demented person may still become aware that the bladder is full, but it is too enfeebled by dementia to exert much restraint. An elderly demented person may have sufficient brain power to do no more than suppress the act of urination for only a few minutes. Being awakened from sleep by the awareness of a full bladder leaves little time to make a hurried trip to the bathroom, a trip notoriously prone to hazardous falls.

Several drugs are available that are mildly sedating and also delay contraction of the urinary bladder. By relaxing the bladder, these drugs enable it to hold more urine before threatening to void; thus they allow more time for sleep between awakenings. One of a number of such drugs discussed at the end of this book is the prescription medication doxepin. Another is the over-the-counter drug Benadryl. A low dose of either may help nocturnal awakening through the drowsiness they cause. They also help the urinary bladder to relax.

As noted in the discussion of urine incontinence, you should be aware that the bladder and the bowels both contract by similar chemical mechanisms. Any drug that has the power to relax the bladder will also slow the bowels. Use of these medications should always be accompanied by some plan to monitor bowel frequency and by preparation to act *before* a serious constipation problem develops.

2. *Hallucination and agitation.* Hallucination is listed as second on the list of causes for nocturnal awakening. It's easy to realize that your parent is hallucinating when the hallucinatory activity begins in the late afternoon or evening. Some hallucination, however, may not take place until very late at night, perhaps not until after your mom or dad awakens from sleep. Typically, a person having nocturnal awakening with hallucination will be awake at night talking, either in conversation with or about the hallucinations. Such a spectacle is eerie to witness. You may watch your parent posing questions to an imaginary night visitor ("Who are you? Why are you here?") or barking commands ("Get out!"). Occasionally there seems to be real give-and-take.

Improving the sleep of someone subject to hallucinatory sleep disorder usually requires medication. There are a fair number of these "antipsychotic" drugs available. Different drugs in this class vary in the degree to which they are sedating. For daytime hallucination, one would naturally prefer one of the milder sedating drugs in this group, so as not to interfere with daytime activity, but at night the most effective is Mellaril (thioridazine).

3. *No reason.* Sometimes a person will simply awaken, as if sleep is naturally over. Your parent may still decide to go to the bathroom, but the urge to pass urine is merely incidental, and not the cause of disrupted sleep.

This pattern of sleep disruption may be a tip-off to the existence of depression. Classically, people with depression will awaken in the early-morning hours, their eyes seeming to open by themselves. On occasion the person will be up and awake for an hour or so before they can force themselves back to a little more sleep (more from a sense of obligation than of necessity). This kind of depressive insomnia is more likely to occur early in dementia, but it does call for the use of a sedating antidepressant at night. These drugs can treat two problems simultaneously—sleep and depression—with a once-nightly dose of medication.

Two well-received drugs in this category of depressive sleep disorder are Doxepin and Desyrel. Doxepin, discussed earlier, has several additional properties, including relaxation of the bladder and stimulation of the appetite. If the constipation can be dealt with by some Metamucil or prune juice, the other properties are sometimes desirable. Desyrel is a sedating antidepressant that has none of these additional actions. If only a "pure" sedating depressant is required, Desyrel is a good candidate to consider.

4. *Nightmares without hallucination.* If your parent is a diabetic using insulin, this cause of nocturnal awakening may be a sign of low blood sugar during sleep, which can cause brain damage. The possibility of low blood sugar, or hypoglycemia, should be investigated before the use of a sedative.

5. *Needing "air."* Sleep disturbance that in any way appears to involve difficulty breathing or lack of air should never be treated with sedation. This is one cause of insomnia that demands immediate medical attention, since it may be a sign of heart disease or asthma. See a cardiologist or pulmonary doctor.

If none of these categories matches up with the sleep disturbance that your parent is demonstrating, it may be a wise first step to look at the medications your mother or father may already be taking. Numerous drugs, including most asthma medications, antidepressants, and diuretics, are notorious culprits for causing sleep disturbances.

If you suspect that one of your parent's medications is causing sleep problems, ask your doctor if mom or dad could possibly do without the medication for a week or ten days. This may seem a bit shocking, but in practice it is a rare medication that is so indispensable to life that the doctor's answer would need to be an emphatic no. In geriatric medical circles, this practice is known as a "drug holiday." By giving your parent a drug holiday, you may discover that the cause of the sleep problem is medication. This discovery may suggest new options, possibly changing the time of administration or switching to a substitute medication. Either option is preferable to adding a sleeping pill to the medicines that your parent is already taking.

What if, after all of this consideration, you remain without an answer? In that case, there may be no recourse but to use a true sleeping pill to help your parent rest comfortably through the night. So far in this discussion, none of the medications recommended for any of the common types of sleep interruption has been a true sleeping pill of the sort that might be given to anybody of any age. All of the medications mentioned above have been drugs chosen because of some special chemical property each possesses in addition to being mildly sedating. Their sedation had more to do with the hope that correcting the underlying defect causing poor sleep would be sufficient to cause a more natural sleep. But what about regular, run-of-the-mill sleeping pills?

In the 1950s, the most commonly prescribed all-purpose sleeping pills were the barbiturates. The popularity of these medications has since declined drastically. Today many physicians feel that prescribing these medications for sleep can no longer be considered good medicine, because of their potential for addiction and the discovery that the sleep induced by barbiturates is of an abnormal sort. More popular now, but also coming under scrutiny, are a family of drugs called the benzodiazepines. This drug family includes Valium, Librium, Restoril, Dalmane, Halcion, Ativan, and Xanax. If you, the reader, have ever been given a prescription for a sleeping pill for your own use, it was most likely one of these. These medicines remain among the most common drugs prescribed in the world and will likely remain so for some time despite increasing amounts of criticism about side effects, again including the potential for abuse and the abnormality of the sleep state which they induce.

All of these drugs tranquilize the brain—not only that part of the brain that controls wakefulness but also the parts that control balance, coordination, rationality, and judgment. The ideal sleeping pill, which does not exist, would sedate only the sleep center and leave the rest of the brain unaffected. In the real world, the best one can hope for is a drug that, if it does sedate all of these centers, will linger in the body only for a few hours. A "good" sleeping pill ought to be eliminated from the body by morning and not hang around to partially sedate the balance or judgment centers of the brain the next day.

Among sleeping pills, those drugs that I find best to use in demented persons are Ativan, ProSom or Ambien. All have reasonably short time frames of action. Fundamentally they all carry the least potential risk of certain effects that are inherent in the use of sleeping pills for a demented person— lethargy, catastrophic reaction, and falling. These agents represent the most conservative approach to the use of sleeping pills, offering a maximized benefit in comparison with the unavoidable risks of confusion or falling. For the demented person whose poor sleep is threatening the stability of the home care situation, a carefully chosen sleeping pill can be a wise gamble to take.

— *14* —————————————————

Bowel and Bladder Control

THE APPEARANCE OF URINARY INCONTINENCE in your mother or father is a watershed event (no pun intended) in their life at home. When a parent who still recognizes and appreciates their own home is prematurely placed in a nursing home, it is usually due to the development of urinary incontinence. Incontinence of urine places a tremendous burden on the entire caregiving team. Problems with laundry, damaged furniture, odor, rashes, restriction of travel, and, for your parent, embarrassment (if the dementia is not too far advanced for that emotion) can quickly compound into caregiver burnout. More than any single factor, the appearance of incontinence threatens continued living at home.

You will have better fortune in dealing with this problem if you understand its cause. In general, urinary incontinence in all elderly persons—including those with dementia—is a function of two issues:

1. How much time will Nature allow between the earliest sensation of the urge to void and the point at which the bladder begins to contract uncontrollably and irresistibly?

2. How much time does it take your parent to find the bathroom?

The first issue involves a change in bladder function that

even healthy older persons undergo. If you know any person over the age of 75 well enough to talk to them about this issue, they may confide in you just how much strategy is involved on a daytime trip or outing. They will explain how they became aware of how much less time they are now able to suppress the urge to void compared to when they were younger. They may surprise you by revealing the extent to which this issue dominates their social lives—how it figures into every bus ride or picnic, and how it may often determine which invitations may be accepted and which social functions may be attended.

As even healthy people age, there is a weakening in the strength of bladder control. The act of bladder contraction resumes a more independent nature, giving rise to its own irresistible urges to contract and to empty. With advancing years, the length of time between the first awareness of having to urinate and the horrifying sense that it is going to happen and cannot be stopped becomes ever shorter and shorter. In peak adulthood, a person may be able to "hold it" for an hour and a half before the moment of desperation arrives. By the seventies, many persons (especially women) will be certain to arrange their daily schedule so as to never be more than twenty or thirty minutes away from bathroom facilities.

But with dementia, the "holding time" may be as short as only a few minutes or even under a minute. This effect of dementia is due to the profound damage being done to the brain, at an enormously rapid rate compared to normal aging. So much higher brain power is lost in dementia that the bladder pretty much manages to escape voluntary control by the conscious brain. The urinary bladder begins to function almost independently, filling up with urine, reaching its capacity, and then automatically emptying on its own. Your parent's demented sense of consciousness may be briefly aware when the bladder's capacity to fill has been reached, but their enfeebled brain cannot suppress what follows next.

Like anyone else, for your mom or dad to remain continent, he or she must be able to get to the bathroom during the "holding period." The difference, of course, is that the odds of doing so with a holding period of sixty or ninety minutes is much greater than with one of six or nine minutes. The distance to the bathroom is the same as for everybody else, but your demented parent must run the same race under a much greater handicap.

To address the issue of urinary incontinence, I suggest that you and your doctor look at the issue in the following pragmatic way:

The first question to be asked: *In addition to dementia, does an extra problem present itself shortening my parent's holding time so that he or she is consistently losing the race to the bathroom?* If so, can something be done about that problem? Here are the most profitable places to investigate:

1. Have your doctor check for the existence of a urinary tract infection. Young people with a urinary infection are usually keenly aware that they have one, suffering a frequent and urgent need to urinate, the passage of urine being accompanied by an intense burning discomfort (this experience of urgency is the closest simulation which a young person may experience of how strong and irresistible a bladder urge to void can be!). In the elderly, and especially with the communication difficulty in dementia, these symptoms may not be appreciated or expressed. Such infections, whether they are consciously felt or not, may nevertheless irritate the bladder and cause it to more quickly go into spasm and empty, shortening the holding time. Before anything else, ask your doctor to check for a urinary tract infection.

2. Review your parent's medication to see if a diuretic had been given prior to the appearance of urine incontinence. These drugs, popularly known as a "water pills," are designed to speed up the flow of urine out of the body. For a body tending to retain fluid, this is good news, but for a bladder contracting in an irresistible hair-trigger fashion an increased flow of urine may be very bad news indeed. A bladder filling more rapidly will also be prone to go into

spasm more quickly and will shorten the time available to get to the bathroom. If your doctor has prescribed a diuretic during the month prior to the onset of incontinence in your parent, discuss the issue and the possibility of a one-week drug holiday.

3. Check to see if alcohol is being used. Alcohol is a mild diuretic, and, like a diuretic, it increases the rate of urine formation. Its effects in this regard are well known, having forced many young and continent bar patrons into the bushes or street alleys when irresistible bladder contractions arrived sooner than expected and rendered them "incontinent."

4. Is serious constipation present? The rectum lies physically very close to the bladder in the human body. If the rectum is swollen full of stool, it will press on the bladder from slightly behind and below the bladder, physically obstructing the flow of urine like a garden hose being kinked. This may lead to overfilling and overstretching of the bladder. An overfilled, overstretched bladder quickly becomes a pathetically useless organ. As often as every ten to fifteen minutes, such a bladder will release a short leak of urine, never enough to empty the bladder, and so frequently that no reasonable attempt at toileting can be made.

If none of these explanations help you regarding your parent's incontinence, two choices of action remain. With a parent who is reasonably compliant and cooperative, you may wish to make an appointment with a urologist. The potential causes of urine incontinence are numerous, and the importance of this issue to your parent's comfort warrants a look by a specialist if possible. If your parent is too debilitated by dementia, however, you may choose a more pragmatic approach and simply focus upon the following issue: *Does a drug exist that my parent can take to lengthen the holding time?* The time your mom or dad needs may not be very long—just enough time to find the bathroom or to permit someone to show the way.

There are drugs that will relax the bladder, allowing it to

hold a bit more urine before it contracts and weakening the force of that contraction. Relaxing the bladder will automatically reduce the number of necessary trips to the bathroom, since a relaxed bladder can hold more urine before it has to be emptied. Weakening the force of bladder contraction may allow mom or dad to resist the flow of urine for a crucial minute or two, and to use that time to realize the need to get to a bathroom and then to remember where it is. But there is a catch to the use of bladder-relaxing medication.

All drugs which have the power to relax the bladder do so because they interfere with the action of a chemical called choline. As a group these medicines sometimes carry the label "anticholinergic." Choline is the chemical our bodies use to trigger the contraction of bladder muscles in the act of urination. Logically enough, any drug with anticholinergic properties will reduce the strength and intensity of bladder muscle contraction.

Unfortunately, as often happens in biological evolution, the same chemical may be used by a living organism for different purposes at different locations. Reusing the same chemicals for different purposes seems to have been an attractive economy in the evolution of human beings, but it has made for problems in the practice of medicine. In this case, choline is used in our bodies not only to make the bladder contract but also to stimulate muscular contraction to the bowels and also to record *memory*—indeed, choline has been called "the ink of memory."

There is no rational reason why the human body would use this one chemical substance to do so many things at so many different locations, but the inescapable fact is that it does. The result is that any drug with the *desired effect* of interfering with bladder choline may also cause an *undesired effect* when it also interferes with bowel choline (causing constipation) or with brain choline (causing a worsening of memory).

Is the risk worth it? It depends on the situation. The "risk" of side effect is just that—a risk. It is not a certainty.

Nevertheless, if your parent has only an occasional accident in controlling urine, common sense would suggest the use of an anticholinergic drug at night is probably not worth the risk, particularly if your parent seems already to be highly susceptible to agitated confusion or constipation. It is not always wise to be too cautious, however. Some demented persons unexpectedly may have a fair degree of resilience to anticholinergic side effects. Even if they are in a confused state, they may not become any more intellectually unraveled by a low dose of anticholinergic medication. Others too have such naturally good bowel function that they can easily cope with a bit more constipation just by taking a bit more fruit or fiber in their diet.

On balance, therefore, if urine incontinence is turning into a crisis situation at home, you might do worse to allow urine incontinence to continue rather than risk a trial of anticholinergic medication. Understand, in general, that knowing beforehand the potentially harmful effects of medication gives you great leverage on the risk of administration. If you know what to watch out for, few medicines are so risky that low, experimental dose cannot be safely tried.

With this in mind, one of two following prescription medications may prove beneficial in controlling urinary incontinence:

1. *Ditropan*, a drug marketed for this use and generally prescribed by urologists. Don't start at any higher dose than five milligrams once a day. The drug lasts for a few hours, and it may turn out that you do not need full round-the-clock protection. There may be just a few hours when incontinence is a problem, and the drug can be given to cover that time period alone. You are much less likely to see side effects with the drug if you use it only once a day.

2. *Doxepin*, a sedating antidepressant that happens to have some mild anticholine properties. If nocturnal incontinence is the problem, this drug, which helps the person sleep longer with a more relaxed bladder, may be perfect. It will

frequently work at low doses (ten to thirty milligrams each night), below its true "antidepressant" level.

If medication is not chosen, or is tried and proves ineffective, the next question to be asked is: *Can mom's or dad's routine be changed to shorten the time it takes to get to the bathroom?* Consider the following suggestions:

- Study the process and try to identify where the critical delays take place. Often the delay involves remembering the location of the bathroom. Try placing a sign on the bathroom door, in big bold letters, that says "BATH-ROOM." Much valuable time in getting to the bathroom may be lost by a demented person trying to remember which of several doors leads to the bathroom. If language skills have already deteriorated too far to prevent making sense of a written word, try using a simple graphic of a toilet bowl. Study how well your parent can remove their clothing, unzip their zippers, and unbutton their buttons; sometimes a change in clothing or fasteners may give them the critical thirty seconds they need.

- Get a portable commode and place it next to the bed if nighttime incontinence is the problem. Your parent may be able to urinate with much greater success if the "bathroom" is only a step away, to say nothing of the reduced risk of falling (a night-light is also a good idea). The use of a urinal by the bedside may prove even more accessible.

- Try a toileting program. If you already have a home attendant staying with your parent during the day, ask that person keep a diary for several days. Very simply, they should check you parent every hour to see if the underpants are wet or dry, *and mark it down*. After several days of collecting such information, you should have a sense of the natural rhythm of your parent's bladder— that is, the average number of hours between urination. It may be as short as two hours, or perhaps as long as four or six. Once the natural rhythm of the bladder is roughly understood, try to head off accidents by having your parent brought to the bathroom on a regular basis well before the next anticipated cycle. Although deliberately going to the bathroom every three hours may seem like a nuisance, it quickly becomes a more welcome routine than incontinence. Recall that demented patients live best when they live by routine!

- Finally, the ultimate solution is to use incontinence diapers. In the last few years, media advertising has made use of aging movie stars in an attempt to recast the social stigma hitherto attached to the wearing of diapers by an adult. If this marketing propaganda effort succeeds, it can only be to the good, for you and your parent. The incontinence diapers do, in fact, work very well, especially the newer high-tech ones that have an inner gel layer. As long as you don't expect unrealistically long dry periods from one diaper, a liberal use of Desitin ointment to sensitive areas may allow your parent to get by with one diaper overnight and two or three during the day.

One might at first think that fecal incontinence is merely the bowel's equivalent of urinary incontinence, but curiously it is very different. The most conspicuous difference is that incontinence of stool is much less common. Persons with a degree of dementia sufficient to cause troublesome urinary incontinence are usually still able to control their bowels.

Fortunately, fecal incontinence is less common, since most families find it to be even more stressful. This problem surfaces in a high rate of premature nursing home placements. Even incontinence diapers—fairly effective for urine, once the person is reconciled to using them—do not work nearly as well for stool as they do for urine.

Ironically, the children of incontinent parents almost always harbor some suspicion that mom's or dad's incontinence may at times be a deliberate call for attention, or in some other way an act of defiance or manipulation. This is rarely if ever the case with urinary incontinence, which is almost always an uncontrollable result of progressive dementia without any psychological undercurrents.

But fecal incontinence? There the conviction is not so strong that only physical factors are involved. Often a significant psychological element seems to be involved in the act of fecal incontinence. Baring those individuals who have a genuine disease of the bowels, fecal incontinence as a pure result of dementia is, in fact, very uncommon. It is so uncommon as to suggest that in many cases a passive-aggressive expression of anger may be displayed symbolically in the act of fecal incontinence.

But don't jump to conclusions! Your mother or father may have a physical disorder of the bowels that you did not suspect or know about. The most common issues to investigate as soon as you are confronted with fecal incontinence include the following:

- Check out the possibility of disease of the large bowel. Talk to your doctor about your situation, and question whether there was ever a diagnosis made that would suggest a chronic disorder or problem with your parent's colon. Specifically, was there a history of radiation treatment, or *proven* inflammatory disease in the past (like Crohn's disease or ulcerative colitis)? In the setting of colon disease, no one, of any age or mentality, may be able to avoid stool accidents.
- Check out the possibility of stool blockage in the colon. Multiple accidents with the bowels over the course of a day may be due to overflow diarrhea. It is not intuitively obvious how a severe case of constipation can lead to diarrhea, but in fact at least half of the cases of persistant diarrhea in the elderly are due to the presence of a rocklike piece of stool caught in the colon. As the colon tries unsucessfully to move this hard lump of constipated stool, it manages instead to push watery loose stool around the obstruction and thence out of the rectum. The natural reflex of both the family and the doctor is too

often to prescribe constipating agents like Imodium or Kaopectate, which mysteriously never seem to be able to bring the diarrhea under control! At times this situation has been known to persist for weeks or months until someone thinks to order an enema and clear out the offending ball of concretelike stool that is wedged in the upper colon.

- Check out the possibility of an intolerance to dairy products known as lactose intolerance. Persons who cannot digest the milk sugar lactose will have abdominal cramps, gas, and explosive diarrhea after consuming diary foods. When a lactose-intolerant individual is also suffering from dementia, it is not realistic to expect that they will understand that feelings of cramping mean that they must soon get to a toilet. Lactose intolerance in a demented individual is more likely to lead to an episode of fecal incontinence.

Common fallacies tend to delay recognition of lactose intolerance as a cause for fecal incontinence in the elderly. Frequently the suggestion of lactose intolerance is discounted with the comment that mom or dad "was always able to eat dairy with no problem," implying that one is born either lactose tolerant or intolerant. Some infants are indeed "born" lactose intolerant, but lactose intolerance can also develop at any time in life, even old age. Commonly it may present itself after a stomach virus.

Similarly, the observation "I considered lactose intolerance, but we tried using skim milk and it didn't help" highlights another fallacy. It is not the amount of *fat* in the milk, but rather the amount of *sugar* that causes a lactose deficient person to be unable to digest milk. One percent, 2 percent, skim, and whole milk each has a different amount of fat, but *they all contain the same amount of milk sugar!* The only milk that has less milk sugar is specifically labeled as "lactose reduced," although usually this information is found on the container in pale and inconspicuous lettering.

The only way to truly know if mom's or dad's problem with fecal incontinence is being aggravated, or even caused, by lactose intolerance is to stop the use of all milk, cheese, cream, yogurt, and ice cream for five days. If lactose intolerance is present, five days without dairy foods will be like night versus day.

• Check out the possibility of laxative abuse. Not infrequently the habitual occasional use of laxatives tends to escalate with old age, as the bowels become more sluggish due to age or medication. Because laxative use has usually been a personal habit present for decades, it may be one of the better-preserved behaviors a person with dementia can possess, as memory loss works to erase more recently learned behaviors first. Even a moderately demented person may still be remembering to take laxatives out of the medicine cabinet, and indeed, he or she may be vulnerable through short-term memory failure to forgetting that a laxative was just taken, leading to repetitive overdosing.

If there is no sign of colon disease, no abuse of laxatives, no suggestion of an underlying stool blockage, or any difference in bowel behavior either on or off a dairy diet, then you will probably need to approach the problem of fecal incontinence according to the program outlined below. You may sometimes rightfully suspect an element of infantile regression or call for attention in the case of fecal incontinence, but seldom can you translate such suspicion into any useful plan for dealing with the situation.

Scolding demented persons only increases their level of agitation, which serves to create disruptive ripples through every aspect of their lives. It is always better not to overreact, because in practical terms it accomplishes nothing. You will need to remind yourself that any psychological dysfunction present is nevertheless taking place within a physically disordered brain, and that the principles of psychodynamics that work in persons with healthy brains tend to fail in those with unhealthy ones. Because of the dementia, it is entirely worthless for you to try to address the issue on a psychological level. Solving the problem of fecal incontinence in an adult is not the same as working on a child's toilet training, and it is likely that none of the behavioral approaches that work with children will work in this situation.

What works is toileting. In the simplest sense, it means taking command of another's personal habits, with the aim of controlling both the time and place of bowel movement as the only practical way of ensuring that it does not occur at more inconvenient times or places. Toileting for fecal incontinence is similar to urinary incontinence except for one important difference—unlike urine, which is constantly being made, stool is delivered by the large bowel into the rectum in discrete, packaged bundles. Once eliminated, several hours will be required before another bolus of stool is available for elimination.

Toileting strategy for fecal incontinence seeks to exploit this rhythm. By triggering a regular and predictable bowel movement under controlled circumstances, it is possible to avoid the problem of fecal accidents. Of course, the induction of a daily regular bowel movement, with or without controlled circumstances, is not an easy goal for many elderly persons, demented or not. This program, therefore, can be viewed either as a treatment for fecal incontinence or constipation, whichever is needed. The essence of it follows:

Step 1: Do not allow the use of laxatives. Most people consider anything that helps them to have a bowel movement to be a laxative, without making any distinction. The word "laxatives" in this discussion, however, means chemicals that irritate the bowels and speed up the rate at which intestinal contents flow down the tract. The kinds of laxatives to be avoided are

- Natural plant laxatives, including Swiss-kriss and Sennakot. The fact that these irritant chemicals come from a plant is a marketing ploy and absolutely irrelevant. Nicotine, opium, and belladonna also come from plants, as do most poisons.

- Ex-Lax, milk of magnesia, Cascara, etc. These agents are effective at producing bowel movements the following morning when taken at bedtime, but the effect can be to stimulate the entire intestinal tract during the rest of the day as well. They tend to produce a stool that is too fluid (making it less easy to control) and with greater cramping urgency (also more difficult to control). As a result, these laxative agents undercut your parent's attempts at bowel continence.

Step 2: Begin using Metamucil. This agent will increase the size of the stool and make it easier to feel and easier to expel. Many people think that Metamucil is only for constipation, but in fact it tends to bring stool into a normal consistency from either extreme state, whether too loose or too constipated. The following points should be kept in mind when using Metamucil:

- Start at the recommended dose on the label, but do not hesitate to increase to two or three teaspoons (remember, three teaspoons equals one tablespoon) if needed. Metamucil is only processed plant fiber. It is not a drug! You will not be poisoned or intoxicated by taking more than directed, and at worst one can only become a bit bloated.
- Take it with plenty of water. Eight ounces is sufficient; taking it with a lesser amount of water leads to a gluelike consistency.
- Use the flavored brand, and don't hesitate to mix it with eight ounces of any other palatable liquid. Plain Metamucil does not taste as bad as cod-liver oil, but it does not have a pleasing consistency as it goes down.
- If your mom or dad refuses to drink Metamucil of any flavor or in any beverage, try Fibercon. Fibercon is almost as available as Metamucil (which is found in nearly every supermarket, drugstore or surgical supply store) and comes in powder, wafers, or capsules. Most people who

balk at drinking the powdered Metamucil will readily swallow Fibercon capsules. Again, feel free to increase the dose past the manufacturer's instructions, reminding yourself that despite the capsule shape, you are only increasing the portion size of vegetable roughage, not giving a drug.

Many people have a misconception that Metamucil is a laxative. Fiber tends to increase the tone of the muscles in the colon and rectum, leaving these muscles over time *better* for the experience—in better tone, and better able to perform their function independently. There is no similarity between the beneficial effect of fiber and the debilitating effect of stimulant laxatives. Stimulant laxatives increase the irritability of colon muscles and, as time passes, leave the muscles in the colon more debilitiated and dependent upon laxative stimulation.

Step 3:   Every morning, with breakfast, have your parent drink one strong cup of coffee. The caffeine acts as a temporary stimulant to the colon and will tend to increase colon contraction for an hour or two after ingestion. Keep the following points in mind:

- Espresso is fine, although a bit more troublesome to prepare for most elderly people. Some researchers have wondered if it may carry a higher risk for elevated cholesterol. Espresso is made by a steam-pressure process that produces a higher extraction of cholesterol from the coffee beans than when coffee is made at the lower temperatures found in the usual American percolator systems ("Mr. Coffee"). If your parent comes from the old country and enjoys Old World–style coffee, I would advise you not to think twice about it.
- Since it is the caffeine that is doing the job, it is obvious that decaf cannot be substituted. Be cautioned, however, that as people grow older, the time it takes to eliminate caffeine from the body gets longer and longer, and in

some frail older persons it may approach twelve or fourteen hours. This means that a person of about 80 years of age may actually be trying to fall asleep at night and still experiencing insomnia problems related to residual caffeine from the morning. Although you should be alert to this possibility, don't assume that it will occur to the point of not trying a morning cup of coffee if fecal incontinence is a problem.

Step 4: Every morning, after breakfast, have your parent insert a glycerin suppository into the rectum, wait between fifteen and thirty minutes, and then go to the bathroom, sit on the toilet, and prepare to have a bowel movement.

Step 4 is key. Every word in it is important and has a solid physiological reason behind it. The opening phrase "Every morning," for example, means *every* morning! People tend to resist this concept, generally on the mistaken assumption that as with stimulant laxatives, "overuse" of a suppository is a bad thing. Indeed, overuse of laxatives is a bad thing, but a glycerine suppository is not a laxative. It is a foreign body— lubricated a bit, but still nothing more than a foreign body. Its purpose is to communicate to the rectum that there is something in the rectum present, something that should be expelled in a bowel movement.

Rectal sensitivity is acquired in early childhood, and it is never compellingly powerful. Stool in the rectum does not evoke the kind of attention that a thumbtack in the finger would command! Because it is mild sensation, rectal awareness can be ignored and forgotten at any time in life. In older age and with dementia, the mild discomfort of stool in the rectum can, over days, begin to fade away. The rectal muscles may relax, learn to accommodate the presence of stool, and no longer react even in a muted way.

The suppository, however, reawakens rectal muscle sensitivity. Even a rectum that has become lax and too quietly accommodating to the presence of stool will tend to come to life with a suppository. As with most stimuli, the more awakening one causes in the system, the easier rectal function becomes the next time. Daily stimulation of the rectum with a suppository actually enhances its sensitivity over time to natural stool as well.

"After breakfast" is chosen for a specific reason. This is the time of day when it is most possible to reawaken and redevelop the infantile gastro-colic reflex. This infant reflex does just what the name implies. When the stomach is filled and stretched, a reflex activates colon contraction and a bowel movement. In babies the reflex works unobstructed by social factors; the introduction of food into the baby's stomach causes stretching of the stomach, and that triggers the colon to empty. Diaper changes follow feedings like clockwork.

This old reflex may have been abandoned at old age, but it remains dormant. After breakfast an adult's stomach undergoes its greatest degree of "stretch." Right after this happens, the colon needs to be stimulated with the suppository, to remind it of the connection it once possessed to the stomach being filled with food. In time, like Pavlov's dog, the colon will start to contract each time the stomach is stretched. Although at some point it may be possible to dispense with the suppository, it will not cause any harm to keep using it after breakfast, to constantly remind the colon of the connection between eating breakfast and moving the bowels.

Once the suppository has been inserted, the last step is to encourage your parent to go into the bathroom, sit on the toilet, and allow the gastro-colic reflex to trigger a bowel movement. This is not always as easy as it sounds. It may take some persuasion to convince mom or dad to go to the bathroom before the urge to do so is felt. Anticipation of an event is a form of abstract thinking, the kind of thought process most thoroughly devastated by dementia. Nevertheless, if a toileting strategy is to be successful, you must find a way to get your parent into the bathroom within a half hour of the insertion of the suppository.

— 15 ——————————————————

Falling

DIFFICULTY WITH WALKING tends to affect most people who have dementia, although by no means everyone. From experience, this problem occurs more often with people who have coexisting medical difficulties of almost any description— arthritis, heart disease, hypertension—and much less often in a person physically healthy except for their dementia. Falling is serious not only in itself but also for the repercussions it has in the management of other dementia-related worries. Unstable walking tends to impact on continence of urine and may preclude the use of medication for hallucination, agitation, and sleep disturbances.

Falling is not often considered a disease, but if viewed as one it would have a fair claim to being a major life-threatening illness. Some studies of elderly people who experience a single fall have shown dramatic findings on follow-up of 50 percent mortality from all causes within a year. There are few cancers so virulent as to boast such discouraging statistics, making falling one of nature's most malignant "diseases."

In part this 50 percent mortality statistic appears so gruesome because falling is not a pure disease unto itself. People who fall usually do so because they already have serious illnesses like dementia. Another contribution to the "mortality" of falls is the fact that elderly persons are much more likely to be seriously injured in a fall than are younger persons, due mostly to fractures of the hip. Whatever the explanation, however, the sobering statistics about falling underscore the fact that falling is one of the problems most likely to force a complete reevaluation of the feasiblity of home care for a demented adult. Rarely can the issue of falls be pushed into the background. More commonly, the problem forces itself into the forefont of issues that cannot be ignored or avoided.

The best way to deal with falling is to visualize the reasons for it and eliminate as many causes as possible. The primary causes are the following:

Blood Pressure Medication: People of all ages tend to be nervous in a doctor's office, and this is even more true of demented persons. They may be not only nervous but outright frightened. When someone is nervous or frightened, their blood pressure goes up. Doctors prescribe medication according to the pressure they measure in the office and will increase the dose according to the pressure found on the office exam. Unfortunately for the patient, once home, and once relaxed, the prescribed dose for an "anxious" blood pressure may be too much for a relaxed person and actually lower the blood pressure too much. As a result, people fall from the upright position, usually after lying in bed, and notoriously after waking up at night (when everyone's pressure is naturally lower) and standing up to go to the bathroom.

The solution? One solution is not to be obsessively concerned about mom's or dad's numerical blood pressure readings in the doctor's office. If your doctor wants to treat the pressure, insist upon being allowed first to buy a home digital blood pressure machine. If the doctor protests that such machines are "not accurate," you should not agree. Although some machines may not be accurate, most of them are, and if your doctor offers only this sweeping condemnation without specifying brand names, it is most likely that the doctor knows little or nothing specific about the home instruments.

You may wish to buy a home blood pressure machine. Learn first how to use it, and then bring it to the doctor's office at your next visit. Compare your reading on the machine with the doctor's reading, and *if the two sets of readings are within 5 points of each other,* consider your machine accurate. Then begin to compile a set of blood pressure readings at home, taken at different times of the day and covering the span of a few weeks. If *your* readings are close to normal, decline the offer of blood pressure medication regardless of what readings are found on the office visit. And, as always, insist on trying the smallest dose.

Sleeping Pills: There is no way to put the "conscious" part of the brain to sleep with a drug and not also put to sleep other parts of the brain that control balance and reflexes. This is a rule of nature. If you violate the rule, your parent may very likely fall as a consequence.

If falling is a real threat, and especially if your parent has fallen in the last six months without a convincing explanation, *do not* give any of the usual sleeping medications that people ask for and doctors obligingly prescribe.

Rugs, Lighting, and Furniture: A large number of falls in older persons, with or without dementia, occur because their houses have become obstacle courses. You need to look at your parent's home not aesthetically but from the perspective of safety. Among environmental hazards, area rugs are the worst. For a demented older person, these rugs are the equivalent of land mines, and they must be removed. Also, mildly demented persons tend to keep blinds closed and lights off (either deliberately or by forgetting to replace burned out bulbs). This dimly lit world needs your intervention.

Likewise, if your parent walks about with hands constantly moving from one piece of furniture to another, you need to see that every chair and table that may become a momentary crutch is solid and stable. If necessary, install some sturdy handrails along the hallway and ensure that existing banisters are solid enough to bear your parent's full weight, and not just the weight of their hand! Remove hassocks or floor objects d'art; create clear paths at least three feet wide wherever your parent will be needing to walk (if your parent uses a walker, four feet is more appropriate).

If your parent balks at any of these adjustments, you have no choice but to confront the issue on your own authority. Trust me that you will eventually take all of these steps. Either you will make these changes before your mother or father is laid up in the hospital, or you will make them afterward.

Footwear: Take a close, critical look at your parent's footwear. All older persons have some degree of reduced sensitivity in their feet, although not all are aware of it. Aging affects everyone's nerves. The longest nerves in the human body are the nerves that extend down the legs to the feet. Consequently, aging tends to affect the nerves of the legs and feet more obviously than nerves elsewhere in the body. The aging of these nerves leaves the legs among the least sensitive parts of an older person's body, and that insensitivity can contribute to tripping and falling.

The combinations of footwear and flooring that are safest for the elderly include:

- Bare feet on a wooden floor. Not wearing any shoes or socks maximizes the "feel" of the floor. Wood is an ideal combination of relative warmth and flatness, although a firm, low-pile wall-to-wall carpet provides a good alternative.
- Low-heeled or flat-soled shoes. The emphasis should be on comfort and stability in the shoe. Shoes should not be excessively heavy. A thin-soled sneaker may be fine, but watch for shoes with crepe soles. These soles these have a tendency to catch on minor irregularities of the floor surface, causing a loss of balance.

- If you cannot convince your parent to try any of these alternatives, at least try to dissuade them from some of the worst habits in footwear. These include walking about in socks, hosiery, or smooth-bottomed slippers. Although wood or tile floors may be fine for bare feet, these surfaces can become treacherously dangerous if walked upon with stockings or smooth-soled slippers. If it is not possible to control mom's or dad's habits in this regard, it may be better to install a low-pile wall-to wall carpet throughout the house. A cheaper initiative might include replacing your parent's entire collection of ordinary socks with "slipper socks," whose soles are lined with V-shaped anti-slip ribbing. If possible, throw out any unsatisfactory hosiery to ensure it will not be used.

16

Eating Disorders and Weight Loss

MOST CHILDREN OF PARENTS in the early stages of dementia are visually aware of some weight loss and not infrequently are more anxious about the initial signs of losing weight than about what may still be only minor and irregular memory failings. People with early dementia usually lose weight for two major reasons: not shopping and not cooking.

Shopping, it turns out, is actually a fairly challenging intellectual task despite its mundane, everyday character. It involves geographic-spatial memory of the route to and from the store as well as list memory for the recollection of the number of items needed and abstractly how they fit together into meals. Ultimately, at the checkout, one needs the ability to perform mathematical calculation. Because of their phobias about leaving home and navigating through an increasingly overwhelming world, demented persons generally are less likely to go out and shop except for items whose daily purchase is very routine—e.g., a walk to the corner every morning for a newspaper.

If you, the child, have already found it necessary to do the shopping either with your parent or on their behalf, you may still be frustrated to see the weight loss continuing. If not lack of food, the next most likely cause is disinterest in cooking and eating. The latter is of some scientific curiosity, insofar as with Alzheimer's disease a neurological loss of the sense of smell occurs. It is known that much of our sense of taste for food is in fact due to the sense of smell. For some demented persons, this loss of smell is a big factor in their loss of appetite and weight. For most demented persons, however, weight loss in the face of kitchen cabinets filled with food is due to a variety of dementia-related reasons that all add up to inadequate intake.

A useful test is to invite your parent over to your home for a meal or to a restaurant, and watch how well the food is eaten. If your parent's appetite in your presence appears good and the food is completely consumed, consider that the reasons for your parent's weight loss may be among the following:

- Too lonely to cook. This is especially true for widows or widowers. Mealtimes are as much a social experience as a pit stop for food, and for a once-married man or woman, eating alone saps much of the desire to cook a balanced meal.

- Too confused to cook. This may indirectly be an act of greater self-preservation than you realize. Each year, fatal fires are started by confused elderly persons who do not possess the spark of insight that tells them to stay away from the stove. Your parent may have already had some untold experiences in the kitchen that have made them abandon cooking.

- Too sick to maintain weight. Maybe your parent is actually eating as well at home as in your presence but is still losing weight. If all the evidence that you see suggests that food brought into the home is disappearing appropriately, have your parent's health checked. In addition to being checked for cancer (which doctors always do for an older person losing weight), your mother or father should be are screened for tuberculosis and thyroid disease (this should have been done already if you followed the directions in chapter 3).

If you dine with your parent and see no real interest in eating, you may be dealing with any of the following:

- Constipation. Mild, everyday constipation in normal persons will not usually disturb the appetite, but in the demented person the constipation may be chronic, unreported, unrecognized (even by the victim) and persist long enough to cause a measurable weight loss.
- Indigestion. This is surprisingly common, but not reported as often as heartburn by the elderly (demented or normal). Frequently indigestion in the demented person will present only as loss of appetite and nausea. These are often caused by medications prescribed by doctors or drugs people will take themselves (aspirin or ibuprofen being two major offenders). Indigestion is easily treated, either by removing the offending suspect (usually a pain medication) or by using a liberal dose of liquid antacid (one tablespoon, four times a day). If money is not an object, you may consider one of the new, sophisticated drugs like Axid, Pepcid, or Zantac. They have few side effects except their cost, and they will usually stop indigestion like magic.
- Depression. Discussed in detail earlier, the cluster of weight loss, poor sleep, and disinterest in life makes this a good possibility. Some antidepressants tend to stimulate appetite even in persons who are not depressed, and these drugs may be a good first choice if loss of appetite appears to play a large role in your parent's depression.
- Medication. As noted above, some medication will cause loss of appetite by inducing indigestion. In these cases, most often pain medication like aspirin, ibuprofen, or Naprosyn are the cause. Other prescription medications may tend to depress the appetite in ways other than indigestion, however. In high doses, digoxin (Lanoxin) for the heart and theophyllines for asthma may lead to a loss

of appetite or nausea, although almost any medication may rightfully be suspect. If the loss of appetite followed within a few weeks of the start of any new medication, you may have no choice but to give a trial "drug holiday" to determine if the drug is the cause of poor appetite or an innocent bystander.

• Physical sickness. Again, as in the case of persons who lose weight despite good appetite, a number of medical illnesses cause weight loss by diminishing appetite. Cancers of the intestinal tract, including the pancreas, are the classic case, although more often I have found simple peptic ulcers causing no symptom except severe loss of appetite.

— *17* —————————————

Coping With Sudden Decline

THERE WILL BE TIMES when a demented person goes into a state of persistent agitation, sleeplessness, or belligerence, not for just a few hours as a result of a medication reaction, but for days or weeks. Not uncommonly these episodes of sudden decline are accompanied by screaming or the display of hostile or violent action. The onset is usually over a few days.

Many doctors will view such abrupt, negative change in your parent as the natural history of dementia. *Do not accept this verdict at face value!* Certainly dementia does get worse over time, but it generally does so very slowly. Sudden changes from one week to the next *may* be due to dementia in small-stroke disease, and perhaps in this case the average doctor's assessment would be technically correct. Remain skeptical, however. Many general physicians are entirely too quick to assume that a small stroke must have occurred and must be the explanation for mom's or dad's sudden deterioration. *Such facile assumptions are wrong many more times than they are right.* The danger in assuming stroke to be the cause of all sudden decline is that treatable conditions may go undiscovered until a great deal of avoidable damage has been done.

In the majority of instances, a small stroke is not the

cause of a demented parent's sudden deterioration in thinking and behavior. The key to discovering the true cause of a sudden decline can be found in the similarities between the infant's brain and the demented brain. Neither brain has the capacity to express inner feelings in language—the infant's because it has not yet developed, and the demented because it has been lost. Both beings will substitute a generalized nonverbal expression of stress in the place of a verbal complaint. The infant may cry, squirm, and thrash inconsolably; the demented person may scream, scratch, hit, or refuse to cooperate with toileting, eating, or medication. Each is expressing a deep discomfort, utilizing the limited repertoire of behaviors at their command. In each case, it is only the emotional side of suffering that can be communicated.

This observation gives rise to one of the most important and cardinal rules of caring for a demented person:

If your parent, previously "manageable," becomes suddenly unmanageable, always assume that there is a treatable physical illness present which cannot be described, except to display behaviorally the discomfort which is being felt.

The search for that illness must commence quickly, because the typical demented patient has very little reserve of physical or psychological endurance. The weakening effects of sleep disruption, poor appetite, poor fluid intake, and absence of medication can bring your parent's state of health to crisis levels in a few days.

In general, the physical conditions that cause sudden decline in a demented person have one common feature—pain. Curiously, obvious external injuries provoke sudden deterioration less often, perhaps because they are visibly apparent even to the demented individual. Elderly persons may suffer very nasty skin tears of the arms or legs due to their delicate skin, yet these injuries rarely trigger a general mental and emotional breakdown.

The search for the cause of a sudden deterioration is

usually a search for an invisible cause of pain that your parent cannot communicate to you. The following causes are sufficiently common to warrant a step-by-step consideration of each:

Step 1: Look for Constipation. Unrecognized constipation is perhaps the most common cause of sudden decline. The spectrum of change it can trigger is fairly broad. Sometimes the result is muted, with only lassitude, loss of appetite, and progressive weakness in evidence. At other times, extensive constipation may produce screaming, agitation, and inexplicably resistant behavior.

You might assume that no physician could fail to notice a severe case of constipation, yet doctors generally are slow to recognize the impact that severe constipation can have on a demented person. In part this occurs because constipation in normal people is so relatively benign that it appears an inadequate explanation for global deterioration in a demented individual.

The major reason for delayed diagnosis is probably due to the fact that even with very severe degrees of constipation many demented persons will continue to have bowel movements, throwing everyone off the trail of the real problem. Families will often deny that constipation has been a problem, and doctors not skilled in the care of the elderly may accept their judgment. Few caregivers are so attuned to the pattern of bowel movements as to sense that the small amounts of stool being passed each day are too scanty to be counted as full bowel movements but are instead just small pieces of a much larger mass of stool that break off just above the anus.

Even more misleading in the case of severe constipation is the phenomenon of paradoxical diarrhea, discussed earlier. The overflow of watery stool around the large, irritating rock of constipated stool often traps both families and doctors into the fundamental error of treating the obvious diarrhea rather than the invisible constipation causing it. Invariably the use of antidiarrhea agents like Imodium, Kaopectate, or Lomotil only compounds the problem rather than curing it.

In every case of sudden deterioration, therefore, a rectal exam must be done to ensure that there has not been a gradual buildup of severe constipation. If the circumstances are highly suspicious, you may need to insist upon an abdomenal X ray, since the large mass of constipated stool may be higher up in the colon than the doctor (or you) may be able to tell by inserting a gloved, lubricated finger into the rectum.

If fecal impaction is the cause of your parent's sudden deterioration, the problem needs to be approached quickly and decisively. There is no time for the more leisurely approach to bowel management outlined in chapter 14. You need to choose among several alternatives:

a. Enemas. Convenient, prepackaged Fleets enemas come complete with small bulb syringes that make their administration reasonably easy, but the small amount of enema fluid contained in these kits is not always effective in cleaning out a large fecal mass. For fecal impaction, an old-fashioned enema bag is preferred. The enema fluid may be plain tap water, soapsuds, or mineral oil—the last two arguably more effective in breaking up rock-hard stool.

Whatever the type of enema fluid used, the key to a good result with an enema is the subject's cooperation. Administering an enema actually requires only minimal competency, but insofar as enemas have lost their popularity in recent decades, most of today's adults have neither given nor received an enema during their lives. If this old-fashioned procedure is now beyond your capacity to perform, you may wish to call the local visiting nurse service.

b. Laxatives. These are much less messy but sometimes uncomfortable. Cleansing laxatives irritate the upper intestinal tract, triggering repetitive spasms and contractions that ultimately expel whatever lies in the intestinal canal. *If there is not too much buildup of stool in the colon already,* this approach will work, but sometimes the stool is so large and so hard that even laxative-induced contractions will not cause it to move. When the intestines are being whipped by laxatives to contract futilely against an immovable object, the result is severe abdominal cramping and pain. If a laxative causes pain, therefore, but no bowel movement, an enema is essential to break up the stool before a second round of laxatives is tried. Most often, repeating the laxatives after the enema has loosened the stool proves much more effective.

Several laxative regimens have acquired almost cultlike believers among hospital doctors and nurses. The combination of milk of magnesia and cascara is known in the trade as a "black and white." This time-honored cocktail is composed of one teaspoon of black cascara syrup along with one teaspoon (or tablespoon) of white milk of magnesia. A small (six-ounce) bottle of magnesium citrate works well enough to have earned its nickname "the Bomb." The effectiveness of these laxatives can sometimes be improved by pretreatment with large amounts of mineral oil, using as much as a tablespoon every hour for a full day before administering the laxative.

Mineral oil acts both to soften the stool as well as to lubricate its eventual expulsion from the anus. It can be a valuable alternative to an enema, but it does carry one serious concern. *Mineral oil can produce a very nasty, fatal pneumonia if it is inhaled into the lungs. Do not give it if your parent is weak and lethargic, typically coughs or chokes when drinking, or is prone to vomiting.* In any of these situations, the mineral oil may be inhaled into the lungs rather than swallowed into the stomach. This risk of aspiration tends to become greater as dementia progresses into its more advanced stages.

c. Digital Disimpaction. The third and final method of dislodging a hard mass of stool is to do it manually. It is a brutish but simple procedure. A lubricated, gloved index finger is inserted into the rectum, with the soft, pulpy part of the finger facing the tailbone. The index finger is used to break off pieces of stool from the large mass, using the tailbone (which can be easily felt by pressing against the rectal wall) as a hard "work surface." Broken pieces of stool are then pulled out of the rectum. It is not a job for the squeamish.

Step 2: Look for Fractures. Hairline fractures of the hip and pelvis are a major cause of sudden decline. These fractures are not rare events and can precipitate weeks of chaotic mental dysfunction in a demented person. As with severe constipation, there are several common and incorrect assumptions that delay the recognition of a hairline fracture by both doctor and family.

The first mistake is to assume that mom or dad could not have fallen without someone having noticed or reported the fall to you. Of course, demented persons rarely report their own falls. Neither, however, do many home care workers. Fear of repercussions can be a powerful incentive to underreport a fall that may well have occured during a few seconds of inattention on the part of a generally conscientious home attendant. Always assume you will not be told of a fall.

The second mistake is to assume that a person still walking could not have broken a hip. Contrary to common expectation, hairline fractures may still permit a person to walk, although careful observation will usually reveal that the walking is not as smooth as it previously was. Even if the weight can be borne, however, the pain remains as a cause for sudden decline.

Step 3: Consider Indigestion. Your elderly mom or dad may well be taking a variety of prescription and nonprescription medications for arthritis and pain, or taking low doses of aspirin daily for heart of circulation problems. Possibly your parent may still enjoy a drink of alcohol with dinner. The causes of stomach and esophageal irritation are legion, and over time may come to cause sufficient pain to trigger a general decline in health.

It is rare to have a demented person explain in words that

a burning, gnawing pain in the stomach is disrupting their comfort and appetite. Again, the most common misconceptions about indigestion include the belief that such a common and mundane problem could never be at the root of such a precipitous decline in health as that which a demented person may be demonstrating. There is also a tendency to assume that medicines well tolerated for years can be eliminated as a suspected cause of trouble. In reality, the *longer* a person takes some medicines, like aspirin or other arthritic medications, the *more likely* they are to suffer stomach irritation or even internal bleeding.

Step 4: Look for Fever.   Mild, "benign" colds and viruses accompanied by a fever constitute another surprisingly common cause of sudden decline in a previously stable demented individual. Generally with fever, a demented person will become quickly and impressively sleepy, due to the inability of the demented brain to function in the setting of even a low-grade fever. Sometimes, however, the opposite occurs, and a "simple" infection will produce unexpected havoc, with screaming and agitation. Included in the category of simple infections are head colds, mild viral illnesses (always called the flu, but usually not true influenza), and urinary infections. The culprit is as much the fever as the infection itself, and even then the fever is usually low grade. To produce a reaction in a normal person's brain remotely like a catastrophic reaction in a demented person would take a fever of 105 degrees or higher. A demented person can go into a state of added mental and behavioral dysfunction with a fever of 100.6. When infectious symptoms and a change of mental functioning develop together the following rules apply:

a. See the doctor within twenty-four hours. This should be done if at all posible, since older persons in general have much less constitutional reserve than younger adults. The elderly generally run a higher risk by approaching a febrile illness with a day or two of watchful waiting rather than immediate action. Older persons with dementia have even less reserve than their peers, and so for them the first twenty-four hours of a fever constitute a particularly critical window of opportunity to prevent serious illness and hospitalization. Ironically, many older persons go to the doctor conscientiously *except* when they are ill and feel "too bad" to go out. Generally, routine well visits are less important than *quick* attention during sickness.

b. Start Tylenol. Give two regular tablets of Tylenol every four hours. Once started, this should be continued for seventy-two hours, regardless of whether or not the fever continues. The only qualification to this advice is that it is not necessary to wake your parent from sleep to adhere strictly to the every-four-hour rule. Nevertheless, if by chance your mom or dad is awake in the middle of the night for some other reason, you can utilize the opportunity to give another two Tylenol on the every-four-hour schedule.

Media fears that Tylenol causes kidney damage do not apply to this situation. If three days of Tylenol could damage a person's kidneys, the drug would never have gotten to market. Compared to this largely imaginary fear is the very real havoc that even a low-grade fever can cause for a frail elderly person with dementia. Fever, even from a simple cold or virus, can throw a demented person into a state of agitated confusion or into profound sleepiness. Either way, the intake of fluid quickly declines, adding to the problem of body fluid being lost by the body simply through the process of evaporation from the heat of the fever.

Round-the-clock Tylenol keeps the fever down as much as possible, and minimizes the amount of mental chaos. Once started, it is important to continue the Tylenol for seventy-two hours before stopping. Success at reducing the fever with the first doses should not bring on a false sense of security; do not stop the Tylenol prematurely, and do not abandon efforts to get your mom or dad to the doctor as soon as possible.

c. Encourage Fluid. Food is desirable, but it is not the key to getting your parent out of a period of deterioration caused by a febrile illness. Fluid is key. It takes the average elderly person several weeks to lose enough weight and strength from not eating to become critically ill. Not drinking, however, is a much shorter route to disaster. It takes only two days of not drinking liquids to precipitate a crisis of dehydration and shock.

Fluid is often the key to surviving a "minor" infection at home. It should be started *immediately*, before your mom or dad becomes either too weak to take fluid or just weak enough to swallow the liquids poorly. If your mother or father seems to choke and cough when drinking, it may not be safe to continue to force fluids by the oral route. To do so invites a process called aspiration, which can lead to pneumonia or even sudden death!

Aspiration of liquids occurs when a person is too weak or too impaired to swallow correctly. Instead of passing down the throat into the esophagus and then into the stomach, the liquid passes into the lungs, with only a feeble cough in protest. Although any food or drink can be aspirated, the primary culprits are the so-called "thin" liquids like water, soda, coffee, tea, or juice.

If your mother or father is weak and less than fully alert, be mindful to any signs of coughing or choking during the act of swallowing. If you suspect aspiration, there is only one truly safe way to provide fluid—intravenously. In the past this invariably meant hospitalization, but with the development of the home care industry there are now a plethora of agencies that will provide the necessary staff and equipment to provide intravenous fluid according to your doctor's instructions.

A second safer method for providing fluids when aspiration is suspected is the use of Jell-O. When chilled, Jell-O can be swallowed as a semisolid, which is a consistency that many older persons can handle better. Once safely in the stomach, however, the Jell-O dissolves back into liquid. Still another approach is to use a product called Thickit, which can be bought at pharmacies and surgical supply outlets. This powder can be placed into any liquid—even coffee—to thicken its consistency a bit. Even this minimal thickening may make it possible to provide fluids safely.

The list of possible causes for a sudden deterioration in an elderly demented person is, of course, much longer than these four situations—constipation, silent hairline fractures, indigestion, and fever. There are dozens and dozens of medical conditions that can cause a frail elderly man or woman to destabilize in the space of a few hours or days. The correct diagnosis and treatment of these conditions is the responsibility of your doctor. Why then, you may wonder, is your doctor not also responsible for recognizing these four conditions as well?

In theory, there is no rational reason why these four should be separated from all the rest. In practice, however, there are several important reasons to keep these four uppermost in your mind. The first is that these four account for the vast majority of cases of sudden deterioration in elderly demented persons; the dozens of other conditions in the medical textbooks occur much less frequently. The second reason is that many doctors are too accustomed to treating these as minor problems, which in young patients they are. Doctors so accustomed to taking these issues relatively lightly are often fatally blind to the potential grief these problems can unleash in the life of a demented man or woman. If that man or woman belongs to *you*, the responsibility will also belong to you, to ensure that these vital but common conditions are not ignored in the rush of doctors to order sophisticated diagnostic tests in the search for statistically improbable diseases.

18

Dealing With the Outside World

THERE IS AN IRRESISTIBLE TENDENCY to misinterpret the behavior of a demented person and an equally irresistible tendency to try to teach a demented person that a particular behavior is "wrong." Coping with problems of social misbehavior in this way will lead both you and your parent to experience a great deal of aggravation. Realize that within your parent's frame of reference at a given moment, the chances are high that he or she is *not* doing anything wrong but is merely acting in a logical manner. As previously noted, when your demented parent does something "wrong," there is seldom any benefit in argument—indeed, argument may only lead to a completely unnecessary emotional explosion that does no one any good. You cannot expect to argue logically from your frame of reference if you cannot imagine how illogical your arguments may appear in another frame of reference.

Demented persons are subject to a great deal of socially unacceptable behavior, the vast majority of it quite innocent from their point of view. The subjects discussed below represent some of the situations which families describe, and these common problems do not form an exhaustive list. The rules of coping with these situations, however, are equally effective with most other situations in which you may become involved. In that regard, the solutions are universal in application, and they all adhere to the following philosophical approach:

All reality is mental. You and your parent inhabit different mental realities. Truth and logic in your reality may differ from the truth and logic of your parent's reality. Therefore, if an issue divides the two of you and threatens conflict, do not argue. Instead, select among the following solutions the one that fits best:

1. If the issue causes no harm, preserve the illusion of your parent's reality for as long as possible.

2. If there exists potential for harm, either avoid the situation or creatively manage it to reduce the risk for harm but without confronting your parent directly.

3. If the potential for harm is real and unavoidable, eliminate the issue by a quick exercise of authority, and afterward do not discuss it again. If your parent mentions the issue, change the subject. Rely upon short-term memory loss as your ally.

Opportunities to implement each strategy will not be difficult to find in your own situation. Consider the following:

Stealing: Demented persons never "steal," at least not according to the definition of stealing as it exists in the nondemented world. A demented person lacks the capacity to formulate a covert plan for the sake of personal advantage. Nevertheless, individuals with dementia are often accustomed to putting things into their pockets or purses while shopping with you in a store. They do not pay for these things, either forgetting to do so or never intending to do so, according to their imagined relationship with the object at that moment. How does one manage?

Possibly, one could cease to allow one's parent into stores, but in most cases this step seems drastic and is unworkable. Because such behavior poses the risk for embarrassment but not for real harm, more imaginative solutions might be to

- have your parent wear clothing that has no pockets when you go out to shop together.
- tell the store manager when you enter the store that your parent has dementia, and set the ground rules for whether you will quietly pay for or return the items.
- check you mother's purse at the checkout, and behave as if it were perfectly natural to carry items in her purse.
- give your parent something light to carry in the store to occupy their hands.

Indecent Sexual Behavior: Presume the intent of a demented person who appears to be performing a public sexual display is invariably an error. It is exceedingly rare for the exposure of genitals to have a sexual motivation when performed by a demented person. Public undressing is much more likely to be a consequence of inability to hold urine any longer, perhaps because of a urinary tract infection, or due to a physical discomfort in the genital area. Sometimes confusion alone prompts such an action, but even then the explanation is likely to be much more imaginative than deviant. Your parent may be acting "logically" in the context of a demented sense of being too hot, being home, being ready to bathe, being at the hospital, or being with a spouse. Assuming that you have already had your parent examined for any sign of genital or urinary irritation or inflammation, strategies for coping with this behavior would include

- using clothing that is more resistant to being removed, with buttons on the rear or the zipper sewn together.
- providing some object to hold that would preoccupy your parent's hands.
- verbally ignoring the situation (no real harm has occurred) while gently reclothing your parent. Use no reproaching tone of voice as you do so, since it is almost a certainty that within your parent's mental state, no reproach would be deserved.

Working: Not uncommonly a parent may still be working when the early onset of dementia develops. Rarely is such employment of recent vintage—most often, your parent may only be able to function even halfway well at the job precisely because it has been a routine learned and reinforced over many years. It is not reasonable to expect an employer to keep a demented person on the payroll for charity alone (although generous acts occur with surprising frequency), and yet you would not want your parent's work life to end sooner than it must because of mild dementia. If your parent is having evident difficulties at work due to dementia, consider the following:

- Talk to your parent's boss. Could the boss possibly find another, less demanding job at the same location? Could part-time work be arranged?
- Offer to reimburse the employer for the "income" paid to your parent. You will likely spend more per hour to hire a home attendant than to invisibly "hire" your own parent, and your mom or dad would never reap the same feelings of pride and autonomy from a home attendant as they would from holding a job.
- If travel to and from the job is an unacceptable risk, arrange for a car service to regularly meet your parent at home and at work.

Managing Money: The psychological "meaning" of money goes very far back into our childhood consciousness. Small children know about money and understand its importance in the adult world long before they can intellectually count and manipulate the different values. The consequence for a demented person is that the interest in and desire for money are more deeply buried than are the skills required to use it wisely; money-managing skills may have disappeared due to the dementia, but not the desire for money.

Demented persons, not surprisingly, perplex their families by "losing" a lot of money. Some is, in fact, genuinely lost, when wallet or purse is forgotten on a bench or counter. Much of it is just given away to strangers, although in the context of a demented person's frame of mind at the moment, the recipient might be perceived to be a son, daughter, or spouse. One might approach the issue several ways:

- If there is very little money to spare, the harm of wasting some may prove unacceptable. In this case, you may wish to remove all access to money by your parent.
- If you can afford to throw some money away for the sake of your parent's pride, you may elect to fill their wallet with loose change and a wad of one-dollar bills. The average dementia patient will not have the mental faculties to count through a stack of one-dollar bills to compute the total. Rather, the weight of the loose change and the number of bills will likely provide the desired illusion of wealth.
- Give your parent a checkbook from a closed account to relieve the sense of insecurity that comes from being without money. Remember to take care to void the area where the amount and signature would be written, lest you inadvertently set up your parent for possible prosecution for fraud.

Driving: In a manner roughly similar to the possession of money, the ability to drive a car in our society is a major determinant of independent adulthood. Driving a car, therefore, acquires a set of psychological values in terms of self-esteem that have nothing to do with the simple fact of transportation. You and your demented parent are likely to find that this is one of the most inflammatory issues to divide you. You will see the hesitancy in reaction time and loss of direction; your parent will see only how well the basic acts of driving can still be performed.

Your parent will be partially correct. As some of the most overlearned of behaviors, basic driving skills can often be very well performed by a demented person. The essence of driving safely, however, is being able to deal with the unexpected. If your parent has dementia and drives a car, the chance of an accident fatal to someone (usually the other person) is very, very real.

If your mom's or dad's degree of confusion creates an unacceptable risk for driving a car, you should not choose to ignore the problem. A demented person should not be driving a car. Having a nondemented person sitting next to the driver may help directional errors, but it cannot help the driver react quickly and appropriately if another car or a child emerges unexpectedly from a driveway. Your options include the following:

- You can try gentle persuasion. You may find the right words to convince your parent not to drive, and usually stressing the danger to others is more effective than the danger to self. This is fine if it works, but if it doesn't, you must move to another strategy.
- You can ask the doctor to serve the interests of public safety by forbidding any more driving. The pretext may be physical illness if that is an explanation more palatable to your parent's sense of pride, or the doctor may simply add the weight of authority to what you have already said.
- If neither you nor the doctor is successful at persuasion, you may have the car imaginatively wired with a fuel cutoff switch whose location is known only to you. Intended as a theft deterrent, this device may effectively convince your parent that the car is not working.
- You can get rid of the car. You may tell your parent that the garage mechanic thought it too expensive to fix (the actual "price" of repairs should be well padded). This is a less emotionally upsetting explanation for its disappearance than saying the car was stolen.

Drinking and Smoking: These two activities do not help anyone's physical health, whether they are demented or not. Nevertheless, both have survived for centuries because they do offer pleasure to people, and that may include your demented mother or father. Because of the greater potential for harm, however, it will fall upon you to be judge and jury of whether your parent continues to drink or smoke. Consider the following:

- If your parent is moderately demented, neither smoking nor drinking should continue if you set your will to stop either. Depending upon the seriousness of the problem, you have the ability to contact the convenience stores and liquor stores that fall within your parent's circle of travel (usually small with dementia) and inform the manager of each store that your mother or father is confused and is not to be sold alcohol or cigarettes. If you have by this time been appointed guardian, you may be on even firmer ground. If you have control over mom's or dad's finances, you can place the shop owners on notice that no payment will be made for these items. However, such drastic measures are rarely needed. Few demented persons are persistent shoppers. Generally all that is needed is to make a clean sweep of the home and notify the few stores that might deliver by phone that no more requests for these items should be filled.
- The exercise of authority is not wrong, but sometimes the issue can be handled with a little bit of compromise. If fire danger at night is the most immediate problem with smoking, you may ensure that the supply of cigarettes is kept by someone in charge and that smoking is done under supervision. You may have your mom or dad smoke with a reducing device that cuts down the actual amount of smoke inhaled if the smoking itself is an issue, or you may limit the number of cigarettes dispensed each day to a measured few.
- Alcohol will never improve your parent's intellectual function, but you may not be able to predict if it will cause or soothe agitation unless you observe for yourself the effect of a small amount of alcohol in your parent. Sometimes one drink is more helpful, and more pleasurable, than taking a tranquilizer; a teaspoon of brandy in

warm milk may be preferable to a sleeping pill. If the effects of drinking appear harmful but your parent still craves a drink, you may elect to substitute nonalcoholic beer for the real item or replace liquor with caramel-colored water.

Personal Hygiene: Demented individuals tend to not wash themselves or change their clothing on a regular basis, if at all. Anecdotally, poor hygienic habits have been considered by doctors to be more suggestive of small-stroke disease than Alzheimer's disease, but this observation does not rest on a very firm scientific basis. In practical terms, you may or may not be able to trust your parent to continue to wash themselves or their own clothes. Even worse, because of their dementia they may resist your efforts in this area as well. You are not without options, however, and these include the following:

- You may not need to do more about the clothing than to make arrangements for dirty clothes to be washed. Some demented persons will wear the same clothing each day, and the only time it will be available for washing may be at night. If your parent shows a peculiar preference for the same shirt or dress, it may help to buy several identical copies, so that some can be washed while the others continue to be worn.
- Admittedly, personal hygiene is more problematic. Many parents will balk at being given personal bathing by a son or daughter, although ultimately the process of dementia will erase their awareness of the social inhibitions of nakedness. That will not be a point you will be able to wait for, however, and the solution here focuses upon hiring someone (preferably of the same sex) to wash and bathe your parent. You may experience less resistance with a hired attendant, since unfamiliarity sometimes carries an authority that familiarly can never pretend. In general, men may do just as well with attendants of either sex, there existing a familiar sense of women as nurses. It

is very much less likely, however, that even a demented mother will allow herself to be washed and bathed by a male attendant, and in her own demented mind, she is much more likely to be frightened and to misinterpret motives and meanings. This will only make for higher levels of resistance and is generally best avoided.

• Some demented persons are like lambs and will follow anyone's instructions. If you are the fortunate child of one of these "lambs," the daily routine of having your mom or dad washed may not be a problem for you or your attendant to accomplish. If every bath is a battle, however, it may be well to rememer how much of what we consider to be "essential" hygiene is a product of our modern cultural mores. For most of the world's history, people did not wash every day, and there is no evidence that daily washing is superior to alternate-day washing. In fact, much of the dryness and itch that many older persons suffer is due to too much drying of the skin from daily showers. Before you resort to drug therapy to win your parent's compliance on this issue, it might be better to compromise. Twice weekly baths are sufficient, and sponge baths may be just as effective as long as sufficient attention is given to cleaning the pelvic area if urine incontinence is a problem.

Remember as you exercise your judgment in these matters that the interaction between your demented parent and the rest of the busy world will never be smooth. In matters of public safety, such as driving or starting fires with cooking, you do have an absolute obligation to do the responsible thing, even if it causes your parent a period of pain and hurt. More often, however, with a little bit of imagination, you will be able to preserve the public peace while distracting your parent away from some unintended action that is of only fleeting interest to them.

Never, however, succumb to feelings of embarrassment or family shame for whatever your parent does in public. If your parent were afflicted with pneumonia, you would not apologize for their fever; if they were suffering from cancer, you would not be ashamed of their pain! So remember that your parent too has a physical illness, called dementia, and that their behavior is not under their control. Sometimes the world may have to bend a little bit too.

— 19 —

Parent and Child: Living Together

IN THE LIFE OF A DEMENTED INDIVIDUAL, there is one cardinal rule: All change is for the worse. The best ally of a demented person struggling to function is stability and routine. Impaired learning abilities can be made to appear much better than they are if the environment cooperates, allowing the demented person the time needed to adapt and cope with one, unchanging set of circumstances.

If stability makes dementia appear better than it actually is, change makes dementia appear much worse than it is. A person who appears to be afflicted with only minor and manageable intellectual failing when at home may display florid confusion, disorientation, and agitation when in another setting. This happens with great regularity when an elderly person with early dementia is hospitalized—indeed, this display of confusion in the hospital sometimes induces the first admission a family makes that dementia is present. Yet it is not only relocation into a hospital room that can precipitate an acute worsening of confusion and disorientation. Not uncommonly families experience the same unpleasant surprise the first night away on vacation or an overnight visit.

To their credit, most demented persons sense that being moved from their own homes will be perilous to their mental health, and they usually resist all invitations to do so. However, some invitations, such as sudden illness and hospitalization, can not be so easily rejected. In these cases, prolonged hospital stays of several days or weeks will inevitably be accompanied by the appearance of mental confusion of a greater magnitude than any displayed at home.

In the midst of such florid confusion, many families wonder if some harm must not have been done to the brain either by the illness or by its treatment in the hospital. Surgery and anesthesia tend to be singled out by families for a disproportionate degree of blame. The truth is that however bad the appearance of confusion and disorientation, *unless your parent has actually sustained a physical injury to the brain, there is not likely going to be any long-term deterioration due to hospitalization, anesthesia, or surgery.* Following discharge to home, you can anticipate that it will take up to twelve weeks for your parent's confusion and disorientation to reverse itself so that they can resume functioning at their earlier mental level. If no physical injury has been sustained, their level of physical function ought also to return to its previous level.

That it takes a demented person up to twelve weeks for the confusion of relocation to resolve is often good news to families who think that the hospitalization experience must have permanently injured the demented person's brain. Taking three months to adjust to a change in location can be a long time for the demented person and the family to suffer. It certainly argues against urging your parent to make an overnight stay with you or your sibling, and it should discourage any well-intentioned thoughts of bringing your demented parent with you on vacation. Likewise, the likelihood of three months of adjustment time should be calculated into any contemplated change in living arrangements for your parent, regardless of the number of other positive points in favor of a move.

Simply stated, demented persons do best in their own homes. If home is simply not an option, the average demented person will eventually adjust to new surroundings, but the transitional months will be marked by what appears to be an abrupt deterioration in the dementia. Urinary incontinence may first appear after he or she is moved to a new home where your parent has no recollection of the route to the bathroom. Wandering may first appear after a move, with the older and more familiar home as your parent's destination when he or she is found to be missing from the present one. Overall levels of anxiety, agitation, repetitiveness, and emotional outburst are all likely to be high for weeks as your mother or father seeks to learn the shape and meaning of this new environment.

Great efforts should therefore be made to keep your parent in the home that is timeworn and familiar. Money and time spent enhancing the safety of a present home is almost always better employed than money used to relocate your parent to a better location. Closeness to you and the family, nearness to senior centers and medical facilities, avoidance of stairs, a safer neighborhood—most children can easily list a dozen ways in which they would be ready to improve their parent's living situation by changing it. All of the theoretical benefits, however, need to be balanced against the risk to mental function that even the best move will pose.

Attempting to enhance the safety of your parent's existing home is not difficult—if you examine the living space as if a toddler were likely to spend a few hours alone in your parent's house or apartment. You will very quickly draw up a list of possible modifications; the following are some of the most universal:

- *Remove most loose objects.* Clutter tends to overwhelm a demented person with a sea of objects to be identified and recalled. Many types of bric-a-brac can cause injury if dropped and broken. Objects on the floor can be tripped over. Exceptions should be made for any items that carry a reassuring or pleasant image, like family photos, although if possible these should be encased in safety glass or plastic laminate.

- *Remove furniture that tips over easily*. This is particularly important if your parent's walking and balance have been impaired either by dementia or by tranquilizer medications. In either case, your parent is likely to walk about by holding on to walls and furniture. Safety will be enhanced if whatever furniture is within your parent's reach will sustain their weight.
- *Remove any poisons or hazardous objects*. Demented persons have been known to mistakenly ingest cleaning liquids or poisons, perceiving them as food or drink.
- *Ensure good lighting*. Replace the lightbulbs, which demented persons never seem to do, and ensure that there is plenty of light. You may decide to purchase automatic devices that detect movement in a room and turn on the lights automatically. Be cautious about daylight. Many demented people tend to draw the shades, and the children who visit often think that opening the blinds to let in more light will prove helpful. In fact, daylight may contribute to glare that is not present with incandescent lightbulbs. If your parent has some cataract opacity typical for their age, their vision may be suddenly compromised by glare during the day. Resist the dramatic urge to throw open the windows to let in the light.
- *Remove area rugs and extension cords*. These possessions are always dangerous and sometimes fatal for the demented person. Get rid of them. Better to leave either bare wood (with a nonskid polish) or low-cut pile wall-to-wall carpeting if you can afford the latter. Wall-mounted wiring can be purchased if your parent's home has too few outlets for today's number of appliances.
- *Modify the stove*. This is essential if your parent is prone to unsupervised use of the stove. The gas company or an electrician can modify the appliance to ensure that your parent cannot be burned or start a house fire.

- *Lower the temperature of the hot water heater*. The typical hot water heater has variable temperature settings from Warm to Hot (often a lower "Vacation" setting as well). Hotter thermostat settings allow longer availability of hot water during a shower but can be very dangerous. Water temperatures of 125 degrees can be easily achieved with the Hot settings. Water at this temperature will scald your parent within seconds if the cold water suddenly shuts off or if your parent forgets and only turns on the hot water. Few people of any age or agility can react to contact with water at such a temperature to avoid a scald; for young children and older persons, demented or not, it is usually fatal.
- *Replace glass doors and tabletops*. Assume that your parent will fall at some time in the home. Replace any panes of glass that might bear the brunt of your parent's weight with either safety glass or Plexiglass.
- *Install safety alarms or locks*. If your parent's dementia has progressed to the point where some supervision is required, make sure that no unsupervised exit can occur by purchasing simple safety locks, bells, alarms, or doorknob covers that allow an individual of normal mental function to exit at will but will delay and deter your parent from disappearing.

Once the physical environment of your parent's home has been enhanced for safety, you can add even greater stability by enlisting the assistance of community resources to help your mother or father function at home. However beneficial, each aid represents some small degree of change which your parent will resist. Do none of these simply because they are available; do whatever your parent needs to have done. Remember the rules of engagement when you enroll your parent for home services:

1. Try to involve your parent in the implementation of home services, offering to respect your parent's wishes consistent with the unalterable fact that the services you deem

necessary will indeed be instituted. Do not give your mom or dad a veto power over your decisions, or nothing will be accomplished.

2. If you require more authority than you can comfortably muster, enlist the help of your parent's doctor.

3. Continue to supervise your folks even after securing paid help.

With these rules in mind, the following resources may represent rich sources of stability in managing your demented parent in their own home:

Informal Caregivers: This term covers people who are neither licensed nor formally trained to care for a demented person, but whose lives have contained a great deal of caregiving experience of children, developmentally affected adults, or possibly their own parents. You may find such a person anywhere, but typically it will be a woman, aged 50 to 65, who may be prematurely widowed and whose own children may have grown up and moved away. Such a woman in our society may have scant employment prospects, her valuable caregiving skills not finding a ready outlet in the commercial world. It will be your responsibility to know the safe limits for such a person—few can manage wound care, for example. Nevertheless, for less money than an agency would charge, you may be able to privately hire one of these persons, perhaps a natural caregiver with an abundance of common sense, compassion, and flexibility that for years will stabilize your mother's or father's home living situation.

Formal Home Care: This is reported to be one of the fastest-growing segments of the health care industry, attesting to the burgeoning numbers of elderly, particularly those with dementia. Home care workers may be hired through an agency. If payment is private, you have unlimited choices of licensed agencies; if payment is through Medicaid or another insurance, you may have your choices restricted.

Regardless of the source of payment, a home worker may

usually be hired by the hour, but for not fewer than four hours a day. The usual increments are four, eight, twelve, or twenty-four hours a day. For a single twenty-four-hour-a-day home attendant, you may be charged only for the twelve hours that the worker is expected to be working. The worker's presence in the home overnight is something of a free bonus, but it is understood that the worker must have a room in which to sleep and your parent must not be disruptive or in need of nocturnal assistance on a nightly basis. If your parent's biological clock has been so affected by dementia as to frequently require a waking attendant at any time of the day or night, you will need to invest in two 12-hour shifts. Each worker will be expected to remain awake during his or her shift, and the charge will accordingly be doubled.

Many children contemplating home care for a demented parent jump to two unwarranted conclusions—that only twenty-four-hour help is adequate and that a nurse will be needed. In fact, a great deal of caregiving can be done in four hours, which will suffice for two meals, personal care, and some possibility of local travel or exercise. Eight hours a day is usually more than adequate if your parent can walk fairly well and is not prone to wandering. This time span allows three full meals, laundry, shopping, and lengthier travels to the clinic or doctor.

Twelve hours may be necessary if your parent needs to be put into bed before the worker leaves but is otherwise fairly safe overnight, either sleeping through the night or able to safely use a urinal or bedside commode. Twenty-four-hour care is never wrong, if money is not an impediment, but its actual necessity is limited to very confused persons with a tendency either for nocturnal confusion and wandering or for sleep disorder and falling.

Rarely is a nurse needed—not unless there is an open wound to be dressed or catheters to be changed (and even then a daily visit by the visiting-nurse service for several weeks or months is a more economical approach). The use of nurses for home care duties is largely limited to the wealthy.

The individual of average means needs to determine which is the least expensive type of worker who can do what needs to be done. In the order of escalating costs, the three choices are

- *Companion.* A companion has very limited care skills and is not expected to do much more than keep your parent company. This may be all that is needed—in essence, a sitter whose presence your parent will (eventually) find comforting, who may repeat comforting reassurances, lend a hand in walking, and ensure against wandering. A companion will not cook the meals, clean the house, or perform personal care like bathing your parent or changing a wet incontinence diaper.

- *Homemaker.* This worker is suitable for a demented person who still has good personal skills—can walk, talk, wash, and eat—but who has lost all of the daily living skills that are essential for shopping, cooking, cleaning, and washing the clothing. Except for cooking meals, this person does not contribute directly to the physical sustenance of your parent; rather, the homemaker is in charge of your parent's home to ensure that it continues to run despite your parent's incapacity for organized action.

- *Home Health Aid.* This person fills the gap, not only performing the essential household tasks of a homemaker but more specifically caring for your parent on a personal basis. This type of worker does all of the things that you would do if you were in a position to quit your job and move in with your parent. They are essentially sons and daughters for hire, bathing, dressing, cooking meals, assisting with eating, changing diapers, cleaning up accidents, and so on. Over time, this person may become one of the most important people in your life as well as your parent's, and the bond between you may grow very strong over the years. Once your parent's dementia reaches the moderate stage, your home health aid may very well become the single most important stabilizing factor ensuring optimal physical and mental function.

Meals on Wheels: This service is available to most communities within the United States. For a small fee, a single nutritionally balanced meal will be brought to your parent's door. Since the caloric requirements of a sedentary older person are not large, you may be able to get by for breakfast and dinner with light, easy-to-prepare foods that your parent can still manage to prepare independently.

LifeLine: Known by a variety of names, these services offer telemetric monitoring of your parent. The plans may differ in the hardware requirements, but most have a telephone check-in with your parent with an agreed-upon backup plan if no answer is received, which may include any response you may choose, from being notified yourself to having an ambulance dispatched. Most of these services offer a necklace device that allows your parent to signal distress from any room in the house simply by pushing a button. These services offer a dimension of comfort for both you and your parent and often are a more realistic compromise for overnight security if twenty-four hour care is desirable but unaffordable.

Visiting-Nurse Service: The visiting-nurse service (VNS) is a valuable community service. Often the VNS is affiliated with a variety of therapy services, including physical therapy, occupational therapy, and speech therapy, and may also in some communities provide home health aid services with VNS supervision. The VNS may be able to provide hospice services for your parent in the final months of life, as well as perform such invaluable services as the dressing of bedsores and the weekly prepositioning of medication into plastic trays divided into days of the week and times of day. In this way, your parent may be able to continue to take medication safely past the point at which instructions on pill bottles can no longer be read and understood.

Adult Day Care: The number of these centers is growing with the increasing demographics of dementia, but it is still not a certainty that one can be conveniently found in every community. These centers are specifically designed to care for disabled adults and demented persons during the day. The staff training, supervision, and activities are more in keeping with the limited abilities of a person with dementia, compared to the itinerary of a senior center, which may be overwhelming and frightening for your parent. If one of these centers is available to your parent, consider trying it, doing so *early* in the course of your parent's dementia, while the ability to adapt to new experiences remains relatively well preserved. If your parent has become familiar with the staff and surroundings of the adult day care center, you may be able to continue to use this resource well into moderate dementia. If you wait too long, your parent may not be able to cope with the center, and after several days of agitated confusion, your plans to utilize the center may have to be abandoned.

Despite all efforts and utilization of community resources, circumstances may develop in which your parent simply must be moved from the home. In general, two categories exist: either to move in with you or to move into an institutionalized setting. Neither is terrible; both options have some good to recommend them, and both have their drawbacks.

Taking your demented parent into your home is a major commitment. For many people, it is the only decision which their heart will abide. It may allow considerable savings in terms of home care outlay, although an honest appraisal must include the invisible costs of the labor and lost earnings of the family member who will be substituting for the home care worker. Certainly it offers unparalleled freedom from worry that your parent is suffering without your knowledge, although freedom from worry is probably one of the few freedoms you may enjoy during this phase of your life.

A parent with moderately severe dementia is hard work in the best of circumstances, and the best of circumstances at the very least means sleeping most of the night. Especially during the early months of adjustment, even that may not be assured. A moderately demented parent may be, for all practical purposes, like an infant whose needs for care may dominate your days and nights. You have a good chance of becoming sleep deprived, irritable, distracted, and chronically fatigued. You may need to modify your home; income may be lost if your presence in the home is essential. You may—or may not—be able to convince your parent to accept a stand-in for a few hours a day to allow you to leave the house. You will not be able to take a vacation as easily as you do now. The care of your parent will require hiring a substitute; your disappearance will invariably lead to agitation; coping with your parent's agitation may negate the pleasure of your vacation (assuming that injury related to agitation does not lead to a cancellation of your plans anyway).

Certainly, taking a demented parent into one's home is an act of love and devout responsibility, but it needs to be examined in the context of the full range of one's other loving responsibilities. It is not a wise move unless everybody in the household understands the magnitude of this commitment.

Invariably there is always some corrupt individual somewhere at any given time who is operating a substandard nursing home and delivering abusive care to its elderly inhabitants. The emotional impact of these news stories is disproportionately great and unfairly tarnishes the image of the large number of reputable homes that provide good care to persons whose dementia-related problems place them far beyond the capacity of family and home care workers.

Nursing home care is generally considered the option of last resort in gerontological circles, but that is not to say that home care is always superior for a demented person. Nursing homes may provide a higher level of mental stimulation than a home environment, where you or the home care worker may be the only other human beings your parent encounters on a daily basis. Some demented persons retain an ability to socialize, utilizing superficial conversational phrases to interact without revealing their intellectual dysfunction, and may respond positively to the nursing home environment. Certainly if your parent's physical health is unstable, they may benefit from the greater degree of nursing supervision and physician overview available at the nursing home, particularly if the home employs its own physicians. And finally, it is best to admit that not all family situations are ideal. Some demented persons exhibit less stress if removed from a home situation dominated by a poor lifelong relationship with a spouse or other family members.

Nevertheless, entrance into a nursing institution after a trial of care at home requires certain inevitable accommodations, both by you and your parent. At home, your mom or dad was likely the only demented person in the house, and the center of the household routine. In the nursing home, your parent can never expect an equivalent degree of personal attention. All health care institutions, including hospitals as well as nursing homes, tend to run schedules that accommodate their staff more than their patients. Toileting, meals, and transfers into and out of bed will never be so closely aligned with your parent's wishes as they were at home.

There are two schools of thought on the subject of when to place your parent in a nursing home, if indeed a nursing home placement is inevitable. One school advocates placement earlier, while your parent is still able to learn and adapt to their environment. This approach is especially appropriate when a facility is selected that offers multiple levels of care, with a spectrum of living arrangements. Early in dementia, your parent may be suited for more independent housing on the grounds of the institution—sheltered housing, from which movement to ever more intensive care settings can be made as the dementia worsens.

The other school of thought holds with reserving nursing home placement until your parent has lost so much intellectual facility and memory that he or she may no longer be aware of home and family. If home is not recognizable as home, then neither will a nursing home room be seen as a loss of home; if family faces have become unrecognizable, then the faces of strange staff members will be no more threatening and no less reassuring. If placement is delayed to this point in dementia, you are less likely to risk a depressing reaction to the move.

Whatever the living circumstance you choose for your mother or father, you must not neglect your own psychological needs. Being the child of a demented parent can cause tremendous stress, whether your parent is living with you or not. Every child who undertakes to support their parent through their final failing years ought at the onset to contact the Alzheimer's Association and join a family support group. The value of doing so cannot be overstated. Not even your oldest and dearest friend can understand what strains you are experiencing without also having coped with a demented parent. Although strangers at first, members of support groups share this common bond and will soon become an irreplaceable source of strength, information, and consolation that you will find in no one else.

— 20 —————————————

Making the Tough Decisions

YOU WILL EXPERIENCE a great deal of psychological strain. As the primary caregiver for a demented parent, you will worry about their physical safety, feel your heart break at the psychic suffering they must endure, and sympathize with their struggle to maintain independence and dignity. Although there are many superficial comparisons between parenting a young child and "reverse parenting" an older adult, the distinction breaks down on one very crucial point—with dementia, there is not the reward of watching your efforts produce a stronger, wiser, and more capable person. Nor will you dream or wonder about what the future may bring. With the care of the failing parent, it is always the past that looks better in comparison with the present; the reward of time is only to produce more and more loss, with none of the reflected glories and victories that infuse the parents of young children.

It is not always possible or desirable for a child to devote his or her life entirely to the care of a failing, demented parent. The needs of the demented parent at some point may become so encompassing that they will far exceed even the care requirements of infants under one year of age. If you, the reader, are single, without children, not working, and choose to devote yourself for several years to the total care of your demented parent, then that is a wonderful and heroic decision, but in practice it is not a choice that is valid for other children in different circumstances.

Dementia is a slow but invariably fatal illness. Its fatality is partly a figure of speech, insofar as the "person" dies before their body does, but it is also literally true as well. As a disease, dementia is more inexorably fatal than even cancer, for there are cases of cancer found early and cured. No case of Alzheimer's disease has ever been cured, no matter how early it was discovered. After a number of years, persons with dementia will die as a direct result of their dementia. The specific causes are usually due to infection, particularly aspiration leading to pneumonia.

Given its ultimate result, it is not always appropriate for a child to allow the care of a demented parent to become the exclusive focus of all family life and energy. You may love your parent dearly, but you cannot jump into that parent's open grave at the time of their death. It is taught to us that the death of our parents will come, and it will be part of the natural pattern and flow of life. It is equally natural and essential to the flow of life that you do not destroy all other family relationships for the sake of providing an idealized level of care for your demented parent.

You must resist the temptation to sacrifice yourself for your demented mother or father if, as is often the case, your self-sacrifice must be involuntarily shared by others to whom you also owe a family duty—your own spouse and your own children. The future life of younger generations needs always to be kept in mind and in focus. Every geriatric physician has encountered the devoted son or daughter who destroys a marriage and neglects the rest of the family by being consumed by a too highly focused sense of attentiveness to a demented parent. Tens of thousands of dollars have been spent to provide round-the-clock custodial care for an insensate human form when that money ought to have gone for the college tuition or the first home down payment of an upcoming generation.

This view may appear harsh, but it is not meant to be cruel. If you or your parent is very wealthy, you may be shielded from the bankruptcy that can accompany the care of a demented person over several years, and thereby be protected from the ethical problems inherent in choices. Most other people, particularly those who are comfortably secure in the upper middle class, should pay special heed to the following advice:

Care of a person with dementia is always very expensive. Home care is expensive; nursing home care is very expensive. Even if you provide much or all of the care yourself, it is still indirectly expensive if you might otherwise have been working or if you lose income by having to quit your own job to provide the caregiving. Therefore, at the moment your parent's diagnosis of dementia is first established, you should consult a lawyer. You need to learn the following specific information to help guide your actions:

What are the Medicaid rules in your state?

If you are not already familiar with the Medicaid program, the odds are excellent that you will be, perhaps sooner than you think. It is imperative that you begin to acquire some detailed familiarity early, long before you come to need it. One of the first items of information you will need to know is that Medicaid is not the same as Medicare.

- *Medicare* is a federal program that goes into effect for almost everybody at age 65. It basically covers hospital treatment and, to some degree, doctor visits and laboratory tests. It was designed to cover acute and episodic illness, like being hospitalized for a heart attack. Ironically, it was never designed to care for the kinds of illness that are most likely to bankrupt an older person—long term, chronic, and disabling illness, of which dementia is only one, although arguably the worst and certainly the most expensive.

- *Medicaid* is known under a variety of different names in different states, but every state government is federally mandated to operate a program to provide health care coverage for the poor. You do not have to be old to be entitled to Medicaid, and you do not even have to be sick. Eligibility for Medicaid is entirely based upon income and assets in the bank. When these fall below certain criteria (which vary from state to state), you fill out an application form, supply financial (not medical) information, wait any number of weeks, and then are finally enrolled in the state's Medicaid program.

  Ironically again, although Medicaid was not specifically designed for old people (large numbers of the poor of all ages are covered by Medicaid), it is Medicaid that usually covers the kinds of care that the elderly need if they are chronically ill. Medicaid will provide personal care workers at home; help with transportation for medical appointments; free medication; and even nursing home care.

As you assume control of your parent's finances and accounts, you will not want to spend money or transfer assets while being ignorant of the Medicaid laws of your state. You will need to know from your lawyer or private social worker specific, up-to-the-minute information for the state in which your parent resides concerning

- the lower limits of monthly income needed to qualify for Medicaid, and how much (or rather, how little) money a person may be allowed to have in the bank.
- whether your parent will be eligible if they have a pension stipend as well as their Social Security income. People have been denied Medicaid, thereby forfeiting thousands of dollars of potential medical assistance, because of small, practically useless pension checks that push their income over the monthly limit. If your parent is in that predicament, the lawyer may be able to help if given

sufficient time before the Medicaid application needs to be submitted.

- how much money may be legally transferred to you and your siblings prior to application for Medicaid, and the time limits for those transfers. Never, ever consider siphoning away more than allowed; if any suspicious financial transactions surface during the financial inquiry that is part of your parent's Medicaid application, it may be rejected, and with that rejection comes the loss of a major lifeline of support!

Realize that you will not be applying for Medicaid for yourself but will be submitting the application in your mother's or father's name. Once approved, Medicaid will be covering the cost of medicines, transportation, home care, nursing home care, and supplies—all of which may at some point prove invaluable to you, and which are *not covered by Medicare*. It is essential to keep your finances separate from your parent's. It may be easier initially for you to purchase yourself the home care assistance that your mom or dad needs rather than convince your skeptical and reluctant parent to pay for help at home, but realize this important fact:

Unless your mother or father is very wealthy or has a short life expectancy due to a life-threatening illness, your parent will almost certainly be on Medicaid at some point in his or her life. Any money which you spend that preserves their assets will delay their eligibility for Medicaid. There will be no way for you to recover the money you spent on your parent's care.

Nearly every demented person of average financial means ultimately becomes eligible for Medicaid assistance due simply to the escalating need for care and the high cost of care as dementia reaches its final stages. The cost of home care or nursing home care can easily reach $40,000, $50,000, or more a year and continue at that level for several years. In fact, the

purchase of more expensive and comprehensive care for your
mother or father in their final years may so enhance their
physical well-being as to further increase the number of
years of life—and of cost! (The "benefits" of longevity in
dementia are debatable on grounds other than the cost, but
more of this later.)

Since you will be given no credit for any money that you
spend on your parent's behalf, saving your parent's assets
while spending your own makes little financial sense. Once
you are bankrupt, there will be no further help forthcoming
for your parent, and there will be no mechanism for reim-
bursing you from their account without the appearance of
trying to hide your parent's assets (which will void the
Medicaid application). *It is imperative that all care needs,
whether for doctors' bills, medical equipment, transportation to
medical care, home attendants, or supplies, be paid for from
your parent's account.*

What to do if your parent has no insight? What if your
parent refuses to spend such large sums of money for things
like home care that they do not feel is needed? The answer to
this very common predicament depends upon whether your
parent has or doesn't have what psychiatrists call "capacity."
This is a legal definition, not a medical one. Everyone with
dementia by definition has problems with memory, judgment, and intellectual function, but the legal issue raised by
the term "capacity" is whether, on balance, a person is still
capable of understanding such things as financial responsibility. One can be mildly demented and still be found, for
legal purposes, to be "with capacity." If your lawyer and your
parent's doctor conclude that, from a legal point of view, your
mother or father still retains capacity, then you have no
alternative but to accept your demented parent's decisions
about whether or not to spend their own money. Realize,
however, that dementia progresses, and that six months' time
(especially without help at home) may well lead to sufficient
mental deterioration to warrant a reassessment of your
parent's mental capacity as viewed by the law.

If your lawyer and doctor feel that your parent is "without capacity" and not able to manage their affairs, you must at the very least proceed with a conservatorship hearing, as well as give very serious consideration to a guardianship.

Conservatorship is a court appointment that places you in the position of being a legally recognized proxy for your parent in the management of your parent's assets. As conservator, you will have access to these accounts for the purpose of paying all necessary bills (including food, utilities, rent, and clothing, as well as health care costs). You remain responsible to the court for your actions and need to be in a position to produce records to account for all expenditures of your parent's money. It is a very broad-reaching authority, but it is limited to your parent's financial assets only. Conservatorship does not imply or confer any other authority over your parent's life—only over your parent's money.

Guardianship gives you legal authority over your parent as a human being, making your mother or father as much your ward as your own child would be. As a much more sweeping power, guradianship will become invaluable as the later stages of dementia appear and you begin to weigh mighty decisions about hospitalization, surgery, feeding tubes, and resuscitation. It is an important power and an appropriate one for a son or daughter to have as they care for their demented parent during the final years of their mother's or father's life.

Because of the greater responsibility involved, the courts confer guardianship with even greater deliberation than they do conservatorship. This more lengthy procedure should not deter you; rather, the additional time demanded should be more reason to begin the guardianship procedure as soon as your parent's dementia has clearly become bad enough to appropriately warrant a guardianship appointment. Do not wait until a health crisis strikes your parent, when no one may be in a position to address legal and moral questions related to treatment. A guardian proceeding is written into law for just such situations.

In my experience, children have seldom pursued guardianship. Although the procedure is somewhat lengthy, the fault does not appear to lie so much in the courts as it does in the children themselves. There are several reasons for such reticence:

- Most children think that they do already have some natural legal status and voice in their parent's lives, simply by being a son or daughter. They are wrong.
- A child may believe that he or she has authority to make medical decisions by virtue of having durable power of attorney or conservatorship for their parent's assets. Children have a near universal tendency to assume that these financial documents not only confer legal authority but also place them in a position above that of the other siblings when it comes to health care decisions. This too is wrong.
- Often there is also a childlike assumption that sibling authority in the care of a demented parent is related to geography—that the sibling closest to the parent, who has assumed the greatest burden of care and has shouldered all of the responsibility, is therefore the natural family spokesperson. This too is entirely untrue.

Perhaps some of the blame for the naïveté of the children belongs to the doctors. Often a physician's informal behavior vis-à-vis a patient's family gives the family reason to believe that they have a legally binding say over whatever is going to be done to mom or dad. Doctors naturally tend to interact most with the geographically closest sibling, while bills and medical discussions naturally occur with the sibling holding control of the finances. Philosophically most doctors sincerely feel that they ought to share the responsibility for important decisions with a patient's family when the patient is not mentally competent.

It is a striking surprise, therefore, to discover at some point that none of this family authority over a demented patient actually has any basis in law. The authority of the family exists while the patient is living in the community, because within the community the family can exercise sweeping de facto power. So long as your parent lives at home, any family member with the power to do so may void the doctor's plan of care by any number of means—never filling the prescription, not giving the medication, not making an appointment for an objectionable diagnostic test, or simply not returning to the doctor. Pragmatically, in order to care for a demented individual a doctor must negotiate with the individual's caregivers. Savvy doctors realize this early in practice. And they understand too that dead patients do not sue doctors, but their families do. After years of wielding such authority on behalf of mom or dad, it is easy for a son or daughter to assume that such power and voice in the care of a demented parent will always be respected by health care workers.

Not until your parent is sick in a nursing home, hospital, or municipal ambulance will you understand that you have no legal standing whatsoever in the care of your own mother or father.

Like most family members, you will no doubt be stunned to discover that within the confines of licensed facilities, you have no legal rights to stipulate any restriction on the care of your demented parent. Of course, as long as you do not disagree or challenge the standard medical procedures, this is not likely to cause any difficulty. Even your refusal to allow some tests or treatments may not cause a problem if the doctors are not very committed to which course of action may be correct.

As dementia progresses, however, the harmonious relationship between family and doctor may become strained by too great a divergence of views over what is appropriate. The first opportunity for a serious conflict of wills between family and doctor generally comes several years into the process of dementia. At the advanced stages of dementia, many sons and daughters have seen enough of its physical and mental ravages to question the value of life in such an advanced state of deterioration. A child might feel that their mother or father may have already ceased to exist as a person, and may feel genuinely troubled by the thought that the only sensibility left to their parent's existence may be the perception of pain, whether physical, mental, or both. In the contemplation of senseless future suffering, many adult children, after years of selfless caregiving, suddenly find themselves unenthusiastic about additional medical treatment that cannot help their demented parent except to prolong a life of discomfort.

One of the great lessons that derive from caring for one's aging and failing parent is the realization that death is not the enemy of human life. The true enemy of humankind is suffering. Not all doctors understand this lesson. Doctors tend, as a group, to experience a patient's death as a professional failure and will conscientiously order endless rounds of tests, medication, and hospitalization with no intent but to faithfully discharge their professional obligations. Sometimes the doctor's motivation is a true philosophical commitment that any existence, even one in pain, is to be preserved; sometimes the motivation is fear of subsequent legal action; mostly, however, the driving force is the routine of responding to each problem with a technical solution. When family members ask to halt aggressive treatment and allow death to come peacefully for a demented parent, they may, for the first time, come into conflict with their doctor or the health agency entrusted with their parent's care.

A request for comfort care—the cessation of all treatments meant to prolong life, and continuation of treatments intended to provide comfort—is not inherently right or wrong, neither moral nor immoral. Rather, at a certain point in dementia, you may justifiably conclude that no recent or future medical treatment has genuinely benefited your parent and that the next approach of death should not be so arduously resisted. If the doctor, hospital, or nursing home staff remains committed to life prolongation, however, you will often discover that without guardianship you may have no legal basis for refusing "standard" medical treatment for your parent—no means of forcing the hospital or nursing home to stop senseless life-prolonging treatments. In many states, even the presentation of a notarized "living will" signed by your mom or dad may not be legally binding on the doctors, paramedics, and hospital lawyers who may be insisting upon actions which you oppose.

In addition to the false sense of authority over a demented parent's life that children too often harbor, there is a second impediment to the recognition of a need for guardianship. The second obstacle usually lies in family dynamics. Initial reluctance to overstep a parent's authority is natural. As the dementia worsens, however, this may be less a factor than a resurgence of unresolved sibling issues. In caregiving situations, siblings usually fall into a natural hierarchy of authority over a sick parent. Geographically close sibs outranking the distant ones; older brothers are notorious for their opinions; younger sisters seem more frequently to bear the brunt of hard work.

Guardianship, however, can be conferred upon only one of the siblings. An attempt by one sibling to step forward as a proposed guardian for mom or dad has the potential to reignite many old unresolved family issues, rivalries, and jealousies. Families whose members subconsciously sense these subterranean fault lines often avoid issues like guardianship as the price for a workable daily relationship. Only a healthy, functional family can select a natural leader to make such important decisions about a parent without risking a legacy of ill feeling. Many families are too dysfunctional to trust any one sibling with the personal and fiscal decisions that will shape their shared inheritance.

Whether its importance is not appreciated or is too daunting to pursue, most demented persons never receive the benefits of guardianship. For such families, the only operative plan is to rely upon good fortune—to hope that mom or dad will die a comfortable death before their dementia reaches the point of inescapable suffering. They will trust that when the time comes, the medical establishment will be sympathetic and not burden their dying parent with pointless medical and technical interventions.

Trusting to luck is not a good plan. Despite all your efforts over the years to optimize your parent's comfort and dignity, once your parent arrives in a hospital or nursing home, or even from the moment that ambulance personnel walk onto the scene, you revert in the eyes of the law to just a son or daughter—nothing more! Despite years of self-assumed responsibility, forsaken vacations, and midnight telephone calls, your opinion will not carry any more legal weight than the opinion of an estranged brother or sister, living in another state, who may not have seen your mother or father in years.

Guardianship offers your parent the only assurance that their welfare will always be the highest priority in all decision making, the same as for a mentally competent person. Mentally competent persons have the right to refuse any treatment, even lifesaving treatment, but not a demented person. If you are of sound mind, you have the constitutional right to refuse blood transfusion while you lie bleeding; to refuse antibiotics while you cough with pneumonia; to refuse surgery while your appendix lies ruptured. You may choose to eat and drink, or you may choose not to if you have decided that a better world lies ahead for you.

The law is different when it comes to the rights of the mentally incompetent, usually stipulating that they do not have the right to object to "standard and usual medical therapy." The law presumes that the mentally competent person would wish to live, even if life means continued suffering. Even though the vast majority of adults when polled report the opposite—that for themselves they would not wish their own lives to be prolonged in a state of pain and indignity—the law inexplicably assumes that mentally competent persons would wish the opposite. This legal language—"standard and usual medical therapy"—cruelly dovetails with the natural compulsion of doctors to be always "doing something" for every disease and problem confronting them. Doctors and hospital lawyers will inevitably interpret the language of the law to mean that "doing nothing" is not acceptable, even if it is merciful, while "doing something" is a must, even if it is pointless or painful.

As your ill and demented parent lies in a hospital bed or stretcher, you will not want all decisions being made to be based upon the most defensible medicolegal position for the doctors, ambulance crew, hospital, or nursing home. You may become suddenly aware that no one except you really knows or cares about your parent as a human being rather than as a patient, case, or problem. You may for the first time feel compelled to argue with your doctors that some of their treatments are decidedly not what your parent would have wanted, and indeed you may have promised your parent years earlier that you would never allow these things to be done to them.

If you wish to experience the purest of angers fired by impotence, then there are few better ways than to watch strangers take effective and legal control of your mother or father and do to your mother or father what they and their legal staff feel is best over your objections. If you attempt to interfere, you may be legally barred from visiting your parent; if you try to sign your parent out of the hospital, you will not be allowed to do so. Threaten a lawsuit and the doctors and staff will become even more insanely attentive to irrelevant details, doing everything to your parent that technological medicine can do in order to strengthen their case that all "standard and usual medical therapy" was applied.

Guardianship changes that. It gives a true legal standing to your objections, allowing you to speak for your parent with the same prerogatives of a mentally competent person to refuse treatment if so desired. If an uncomfortable test has no purpose, you can forbid it. No more hospitalizations? No more intravenous? No tube feeding through the nose? As guardian you now are in authority and can speak for your parent. Your "no" carries weight, and it will be honored. A living will that contains the same instructions can never be relied upon to carry the same weight as the directives of a court-appointed guardian.

You might think that the exercise of guardianship powers would be met with resentment by the doctors and staff. Surprisingly not. You will discover that doctors and staff are, as individuals, likely to be genuinely sympathetic to your objections. Guardianship can defuse the confrontation between family and physician because it offers to the doctors and staff immunity from the perceived legal consequences of having "done nothing" about a serious problem. The very health care practitioners who would have thwarted you when you were not the guardian will often be relieved to have you appointed guardian, after which appointment they no longer have the full weight of responsibility for tough ethical decisions. It may serve as a surprising revelation to see how differently doctors, nurses, and staff feel about the end stages of human life with dementia when they are free to express their personal rather than professional opinions.

The remaining chapters deal with tough decisions that will need to be made if your parent should survive long enough to experience the final stages of dementia. They advise when you should consider saying no to medical technology offered for life prolongation. As the mature child of a mother or father with advanced dementia, you will at this stage typically be needed less to provide care to your parent and more to define the philosophy, objectives, and limits of care being provided by others. You will need to prepare yourself with the necessary legal procedures to enable you to make these painful decisions. Your final evolution as a caregiver will be the point at which you raise your voice in authority to speak for the lost voice of your mother or father.

21

Problems at the End of Life

AMONG THE COMMON DISEASES of the elderly, medical science has treatments for every illness that are superior to the treatment doctors can offer for dementia. The implication of this statement is that it is more probable that your parent's death will be due to the late complications of dementia itself rather than a result of some other associated illness. This is unfortunate, because in the end most illnesses bring about a more merciful death than does advanced dementia. The final stages of dementia bring not only a great deal of physical discomfort and indignity but also a collection of difficult moral and ethical decisions.

These difficult questions touch upon the meaning and value of life—whether the essence of life in a human being is the life of the body or that of the mind, and thereby whether medical treatment or tube feeding to sustain the body ought to be initiated if mind and personality have been reduced to rubble. Compared to dying by sudden heart attack or rapidly advancing cancer, dying as a result of dementia is a far more torturous process for patient and family alike.

By the time that either Alzheimer's dementia or small-stroke dementia has reached its final stages, your mom or dad will have undergone a profound physical transformation. A person afflicted with advanced dementia is as different from one with early dementia as the latter is from a normal person!

In the early stages of the disease, your parent's problems were primarily derived from a failure of short-term memory and higher intellectual functions. In appearance, however, mom or dad with early dementia was still recognizable as mom or dad. Dad's anger may have been too frequent or inappropriate, but the person displaying the anger was still dad.

By the final stages of dementia, a great deal of the agitation, screaming, hallucination, and confusion may have subsided. You may find that your parent needs less tranquilizer medication as well. These changes are welcome, but they are also bittersweet, since easier behavioral management is probably due to a much reduced mind no longer able to generate these emotions or reactions.

As dementia progresses there is less physical resemblance to the person who used to exist. Eventually the disease damages brain tissue beyond the cortex, which generates the "higher" human qualities of intellect and personality. Brain damage of advanced dementia seem to extend "deeper" into the older and more primitive levels of brain. Damage at these sites begins to accumulate in significant amounts, affecting posture, movement, muscle tone, balance, and swallowing. The human body begins to lose its physical ability to move, react, or interact, until finally there develops a generalized physical deterioration of the body that will ultimately cause death.

It is improbable that you yourself will be still be performing the bulk of actual hands-on caring unless you possess the skills of a nurse, either by training or natural instinct. Nevertheless, there are some things you need to know in order to intelligently monitor the actions of those caring for your parent.

Contracture: Even when relaxed, muscles always exist in a state of tension—what we call muscle "tone." Weak people who exercise little may have poor resting muscle tone; athletes have heightened tone. The range of differences in muscle tone is evident to the untrained eye every summer at poolside or the beach.

Muscle tone is actually controlled by the brain. The brain can increase tone during emotional stress or reduce it during periods of relaxation. This control is not achieved by a single "dial" as you might imagine, being "turned" one way or the other. In fact, the brain has two independent systems to control tone—turning on one system increases muscle tone; turning on the other reduces it. Turning on both equally gives normal tone.

Whatever the degree of muscle tone in a healthy person, it is always balanced. The tone of the muscles that flex the arm, for example, is equal to the tone of the muscles that extend the arm. Advanced dementia damages the balance of this finely regulated system of muscle control. Dementia damage to the brain causes disproportionate weakening of the systems that relax, leaving dominant the systems that *tighten* muscle tone. Additionally, dementia is also biased in the muscle groups it affects, damaging systems for the *flexor muscles* more than the relaxational systems for the extensor muscles.

As a result of this pattern of injury, all muscle groups increase their resting state of tension, but the muscles that flex the body increase their tone more so than any other muscles. These flexor muscle groups are the ones that draw the arms up toward the front of the chest, bend the body forward at the waist, and bend the legs at the knees. When all of the flexor muscle groups are at their maximal tone, the shape of the human body is like a closed ball, or, as some have seen it, similar to the curled fetal position which the fetus occupies in its mother's womb.

The consequences of assuming this flexed or fetal position can be seen at the elbows, hips, and knees, where persistent tightness of these joints develops. Attempts to stretch out these joints will be met by tension and resistance.

Initially you may be able to stretch these joints by brute force, which is usually accompanied by pain for your mother or father. Within a few hours of being stretched out, however, the elbow, hip, and knee joints will be retightened back into their flexed, fetal position by the increased tone of the flexor muscles. Eventually the battle is lost to the dementia, as the pain of stretching and the rapidity of relapse render the exercise cruel and futile.

Curiously, the postural changes of dementia are also noted as a part of normal aging, although to a milder degree. Observation of the very old commonly shows a mild version of the flexed fetal position, with a tendency to hold the arms up to the body, slightly bent at the elbows. The stooped posture of many elderly will also, on careful examination, be seen to be due in part to a tendency to bend forward at the hips, and often the knees are a bit bent as well.

The body positional changes of dementia are much more malignant, however, than any changes present in a normal person of advanced age. Forward bending and stiffening at the hip throws the body's center of gravity dangerously, greatly enhancing the chances of falling. Tightening of the knees can quickly render a person unable to walk, it taking only about 15 degrees of flexion at the knee to obliterate the ability to stand upright, making a wheelchair mandatory. Development of the full-blown fetal position makes even a wheelchair impossible to manage, and leaves no alternative to the victim but permanent confinement to bed.

The development of a tight, contracted fetal position is the most uncomfortable end result of the increase in muscle tone that accompanies dementia. Its ultimate consequence is to force the individual to become bedbound. Without a hospital bed that can be cranked into various positions your mother or father may only be able to lie on the left or right side, unable to turn without help. With a hospital bed, you may be better able to adjust the bed to conform to the curvature of your parent's back. Although hospital beds are not famous for their comfortable mattresses, their greater flexibility in positioning usually outweighs this consideration, especially when changing body position every few hours to prevent bedsores becomes a paramount concern.

Decubitus Ulcers: The end result of a permanent fetal body position is to bring different parts of the body into unfamiliar physical contact with the surfaces of chairs or mattresses. These body parts were never naturally endowed with a sufficient padding of fat to resist the pressure effects of surface contact. Many of these body areas may now become damaged by pressure injury unless special padding solutions can be found for each area.

"Bedsore" is an old and outdated term for what are now called decubitus ulcers—ulcers of the skin caused by too prolonged resting pressure at one site. Decubitus ulcers may exist in various stages according to the depth of the ulcer. At its earliest stage, a decubitus ulcer may not even be an ulcer at all—rather, it is an area of tender redness that looks like a rash. But as pressure injury continues, a true ulcer appearance will develop. Initially the ulcers are very shallow, as if the surface layer of skin were rubbed off. Deeper ulcers can develop quickly, however, and as they deepen they will sequentially expose the underlying fat beneath the skin, followed by the muscle beneath the fat, and finally the bone beneath the muscle. These ulcers are painful at all stages and depths—even before the true ulcers develop. The deeper ulcers often become infected with serious types of bacteria that may impart a black gangrenous appearance to the wound, oozing pus, and a foul odor that can fill the entire room with a sickening stench.

Decubitus ulcers develop when pressure on the skin is present long enough to prevent blood from reaching the area. Pressure on the skin from a mattress or chair seat acts like a tourniquet on the arm, squeezing small blood vessels shut so that no circulation can reach the area. Were this happening to an arm or leg, you would see the purplish color of the limb being strangled by a tourniquet and could take action before the tissue dies—but you can't see the pressure injury to skin upon which a person sleeps or sits until the damage is done. Although skin is more tolerant of poor circulation and low oxygen than vital organs like the heart or brain, nevertheless no living tissue can be too long without its flow of blood. After a too lengthy interruption of its circulation, skin and muscle will die of asphyxiation. The dead tissue sloughs off, and the ulcer is born.

Why do not we all get decubitus ulcers? Because there is a built-in timing mechanism in our brains which unconsciously works to keep shifting our body position. While awake we may be momentarily aware of being uncomfortable in one position; we may suddenly stand up and mention that we are "tired of sitting," or we may squirm a bit in our chair. Even during sleep, we toss, turn, and move position not as a reflection of a poor quality sleep but in fact to prevent any prolonged pressure on any one skin site.

With advanced dementia comes damage to the brain's clockwork system for changing position—our natural rotisserie. Persons with advanced dementia do not change body position very much, if at all. Where they sit or lie is where they will stay, until moved. Loss of muscle strength, muscle tightness, and flexion position all contribute to this immobility, but it is the dementia itself that does most of the damage by diminishing the body's natural habit of automatic, unconscious repositioning.

The development of decubitus ulcers will occur when the conditions are favorable. Although deformity of the body's shape by contracture is not a necessary prerequisite to the development of decubitus ulcers, it does contribute to making the problem worse. There is no absolutely necessary precondition, but the more of the following conditions your parent has in addition to dementia, the more likely it is that an ulcer will develop:

- limited mobility.
- poor circulation due to heart disease or hardening of the arteries.
- sitting on firm chairs or sleeping on firm mattresses for long periods. In a very vulnerable individual with multiple risk factors, a decubitus ulcer can develop with as little as two hours of unprotected pressure against a firm cushioned surface.
- being underweight. This reduces the amount of natural cushioning from body fat and makes the skin and muscle being squeezed between bone and mattress even more vulnerable.
- being malnourished. This usually, but not always, goes hand in hand with being thin, but even slightly stocky elderly persons can be in a temporary state of protein and calorie deprivation. This deprivation will impede the ability of the body to repair minor pressure damage that might otherwise have gone unnoticed, and lead to more rapid advance of ulceration.
- diabetes, which independently impedes circulation and inhibits wound healing.
- urinary incontinence. Moist skin deteriorates faster than dry skin under pressure and can become more easily infected.

The typical location for a decubitus ulcer, or bedsore, is over a bony prominence. If sitting upright is the position maintained too long, the location will be on the buttocks overlying the bones you feel on each side if you sit down on a hard floor or sidewalk. If sitting up in bed at a forty-five-degree angle is your parent's preferred position then the tip of the tailbone, or coccyx, will take the brunt of the body's weight and be at risk for a pressure ulcer.

Other common sites include the heels, ankle bones, and hips in bedbound persons, and the very center of the back in persons with some curvature of the spine, and even at the calves and knees in individuals sitting for long periods in wheelchairs with ill-fitting leg supports. In practice, however, a demented person can develop a pressure sore at any spot in the body if pressure is too long applied; individuals with unusual body contortions from contracture may develop sores on their fingers, head, or the ribs.

The treatment of pressure sores once they develop will certainly involve the physician, and possibly a surgeon as well if the ulcer is deep and filled with dead or infected tissue that needs to be surgically cleaned out. You may wish to have a nurse do a daily change of the dressing, although only the deepest ulcers absolutely need a nurse's expertise. Care of the simpler, shallow ulcers is not much different than taking care of a child's scraped knee—wash gently, pat dry, apply the prescribed cream, and cover the wound, usually with a four-inch gauze square held in place by paper tape (which is less likely to cause a skin allergy than traditional adhesive tape).

Although you may need to treat ulcers in your parent, your principal role as the son or daughter of a demented parent is to prevent pressure ulcers rather than treat them. The prevention of pressure ulcers of the skin requires the following steps:

- Make provision for a change in position not less frequently than every two hours. If your parent is homebound (which by this time is likely true), buy a clock that can be programmed to ring every two hours during the day until your home care worker understands that you are absolutely serious about this procedure, and that two hours means two hours. If your parent is not bedbound, do the same procedure, and insist that your parent's position be changed to whatever degree is possible (even assisted standing in place will take some momentary pressure off the buttocks and allow some circulation to return).
- Go to a surgical supply house and purchase either a gel cushion (the best, but more expensive) or a donut inflata-

ble cushion (cheap and also very effective) to be used on any chair or wheelchair seat that your parent uses. Do not, however, let space-age technology lull you into a false sense of security. Keep running the alarm every two hours! Nothing can substitute for a change in position.

- If your parent is sleeping through the night and incontinent, any skin area likely to be wet overnight from urine should be liberally covered with Desitin cream to provide a moisture barrier.
- If possible, buy the best incontinence diapers you can, like Attends or Depends. They have a gel-based technology that absorbs the urine into the substance of the diaper, where it chemically reacts to form a gel, keeping the inner lining of the diaper drier.
- Again if money is a problem, you can purchase a cheap foam "egg-crate" mattress cover for the bed, although this does not work nearly as well as an alternate-pressure air mattress. These fit over the regular mattress and are connected to an air pump that alternately inflates and deflates different air cells in the mattress. Even if your parent lies perfectly motionless, the mattress will rotate the weight-bearing skin areas, giving each area a chance to breathe.

For as long as your parent is at home and under your care, you may have fairly good control of the situation. But take heed of the following prophecies when it comes to the possible hospitalization of your parent:

- After months of careful attention and clean skin, your parent will likely develop his or her first decubitus ulcer within forty-eight hours of being hospitalized.
- The doctors will not notice a pressure sore if it is on the back until it is deep enough to almost reach the underlying fat (and perhaps even the muscle).
- No one will mention the ulcer to you until shortly before it is time to take your parent home.

Why does this sequence of events happen again and again to demented people admitted to hospitals? The basic problem is that hospitals and doctors have as their focus the acute, possibly life-threatening illness for which the demented person was admitted to the hospital. During the first few days, doctors and staff are preoccupied with the function of vital organs and more obvious and compelling symptoms such as high fever, shortness of breath, intestinal bleeding, and heart irregularities. In such a milieu, preventative care of the skin is invariably forgotten.

This neglect comes at an unfortunate time, since the skin of a sick person is often especially vulnerable to pressure sores. With many types of sudden illness, there is an automatic reduction of circulation to the skin. This reduction of skin circulation causes sick people to so often appear pale. When a sick person has pale skin, it means that the circulation of that skin is even poorer than it would ordinarily be, and therefore it will take even less time than usual for a pressure ulcer to develop.

Further delay in the recognition of pressure ulcers comes about because patients in hospitals invariably lie on their backs in hospital beds. Doctors rarely turn patients over to inspect the back during their bedside examinations. As a result, a full-blown decubitus ulcer can become quickly established by the time that your parent is just beginning to respond to treatment and feel better.

It is probably safe to assume that your parent will develop a pressure sore while hospitalized unless *you* make it your personal mission to prevent it (assuming, of course, that you too do not succumb to the hypnotic effect of the major illness and forget about skin ulcers). The steps to take are the following:

- If you can afford private duty nursing, order it, and instruct the nurse that the prevention of decubitus ulcers is a high priority for you. Do not expect, however, that your insurance or Medicare will cover private duty nursing unless there is some other justification for it as well. Insurance generally does not consider the prevention of decubitus ulcers to be a sufficient reason for a private duty nurse, so make this decision based upon your ability to pay.

- During visiting hours, *politely* either ask a nurse for permission to roll your parent onto the side yourself or ask one of the nurses to help you. Tell the nurse you want to look at the skin between the folds of the buttocks and over the low back to make sure a pressure sore is not developing. A simple IV or bladder catheter should not prevent this maneuver. If your parent is lying in an ICU or CCU bed with special monitoring devices or has had major surgery, you may not be able to do so for several days. Even if your request cannot be honored, it will immediately convey to the staff that you are unusually knowledgeable about decubitus ulcers and might also be unusually troublesome if one develops in your mother or father. The ability to be always courteous with staff while simultaneously causing them to experience subconscious angst is a valuable social skill.
- Specifically ask your doctor to order an "alternate pressure air mattress." If it does not appear on your parent's bed within eight hours, ask to speak first to the head nurse and then if necessary the supervisor or hospital administrator. Realize that you must act quickly. Although the ulcer appears several days later as the dead tissue peels off, the initial circulatory injury is likely to happen in the first or second day. Do not wait until you see an ulcer forming, the way doctors usually do, for by then underlying tissue is already dead and ulcer formation cannot be averted.

At home, you have a very high order of confidence that these steps will prevent pressure ulcers. In the hospital, your confidence must always be less, in part because you are forced to a peripheral role. Nevertheless, you can still reverse the odds of ulcer formation to your favor by following these guidelines.

A discussion of the prevention of decubitus ulcers naturally leads into a discussion of the third major complication of advanced dementia—aspiration, and the associated malnutrition that occurs as eating and drinking become compromised. Although contractures may predispose to decubitus ulcer formation, imaginative padding and frequent positioning will often allow you to compensate for the contracture. Malnutrition, however, is a more daunting obstacle, and one whose presence makes it nearly impossible to prevent or heal ulcers despite the most meticulous personal care and attention. Nevertheless, by careful padding and positioning, you may be able to postpone the appearance of refractory decubitus ulcers until such a time in the course of dementia that death may be near and your parent's level of pain awareness not much more than it would be in a dream.

Aspiration: The same process of deep brain destruction by dementia that leads to contracture development and devastates the ability to walk will usually affect the swallowing mechanism at approximately the same time. Like walking, swallowing is an unconscious activity whose complexity and delicate choreography go unappreciated in everyday life. The essence of the act is to propel food down the throat and into the esophagus, with split-second timing needed to close the airway passages just as the food bolus passes by. If this coordination is off in its timing, little bits of food, liquid, or saliva will detour into the airways with each swallow. This is the process called aspiration.

Most people have experienced a momentary failure of their own swallowing mechanism, when a bit of food or drink "goes down the wrong pipe." The result is an irresistible paroxysm of coughing and choking if the episode is minor; if major, the result may be death unless luck or a Good Samaritan comes to the rescue. The cough-and-choke is a lifesaving reflex built into our bodies as a backup system should the swallowing mechanism fail. The relative rarity of aspiration episodes, even in crowded restaurants full of dining patrons, is a testimonial to the remarkable accuracy of the swallowing mechanism in healthy persons.

Demented persons are afflicted in two ways:

- The dementia process invariably affects the reliability and efficiency of the swallowing mechanism. By advanced dementia, it is safe to assume that your parent is intermittently mis-swallowing foods, liquids, and saliva.
- The dementia process variably affects the backup cough-and-choke reflex. In some persons, this reflex is abolished, meaning that aspiration episodes may not be felt by your parent or be recognized by you. Most demented persons, however, retain some of this gag reflex, although its vigor and intensity varies from near normal to very muted and of limited protection.

Dysfunction with the swallowing mechanism and possible associated degradation of the cough reflex make demented persons susceptible to choking on food and pneumonia—the latter due to the eventual penetration of germ-laden saliva mixed with food or drink that manages to find its way into the lungs. In the natural world, divorced from high-tech medicine, the consequences of swallowing dysfunction are the natural means of death for the vast majority of elderly persons with dementia. Malnutrition due to difficulty with eating and reduced intake, combined with repeated seeding of the lungs with germs, makes death by pneumonia the "natural" expected means of death for a demented person.

There are several strategies in feeding that can temporarily compensate for a deteriorating swallowing mechanism and thereby postpone the onset of "aspiration pneumonia." The following checklist should be studied if your parent's dementia has reached this level of severity:

- If your parent is coughing or choking with eating, study which foods are causing the trouble. It may be solids if the pieces are too large or the dentures are too ill-fitting to allow proper mastication. If so, cut the pieces finer, and if you can find a dentist to attend your parent despite the dementia (such dentists are rare!), have the dentures fixed. If this proves ineffective, change to a puree diet, which is the easiest to manage with dementia. Avoid the apparent convenience of baby food—for the amounts you will need, it is an expensive choice to make, and many are too rich in salt to be healthy for an older person's heart and blood pressure. It is an easy step to simply puree in a blender the same food that would have been cooked and placed on the dish had your parent been able to eat normally.
- Beware of liquids. It is usually liquids that are the most difficult food consistency to swallow and the one most likely to be aspirated. Of course, one cannot long survive without liquids, but several imaginative strategies can be developed. The use of Jell-O is an excellent way to provide liquid in a semisolid state that is easy to swallow but reverts to liquid in the stomach. It can be purchased sweetened or in a nonsugar variant for diabetics. Another strategy is to thin the pureed foods slightly with water or juice so that each swallow of pureed food carries a bit of extra fluid. Finally, additives like Thickit can be added to any liquid in varying amounts to thicken slightly the consistency of some drinks that your parent may prefer, like coffee.
- Never feed your parent unless they are in the fully upright position. Preferably this should be done out of bed and in a chair. Sitting *almost* upright in a hospital bed already begins to noticeably increase the risk of aspiration.
- Never feed your parent unless they are fully awake and unless you are sure that your parent is paying attention to eating. If tranquilizer drugs are leaving your parent too dopey to sit up and pay attention to eating, stop the drugs.

- Try moistening your parent's mouth with an artificial moisturizer. One such "artificial saliva" is a product called Salivart, which provides a longer period of moistening of the mouth than is possible with water or juices. The use of such a product before feeding may help the act of swallowing.
- You may discover a difference between the right and left side of the mouth. The swallow mechanism may be better on one side and worse on the other. If you believe that you can see a difference, make it a routine when spoon-feeding to tilt the spoon so that it delivers the contents to the better side.
- If your parent chokes or coughs, stop the feeding, but do not perform any of those outdated and discredited actions like patting your parent on the back. If you suspect that food has already entered the airway, perform a Heimlich maneuver. If you can hear a noisy cough, choke, or gasp, then you know the airway must be open. If you see your parent struggling but cannot hear a sound, then you must presume that your parent is truly choking and immediately repeat the Heimlich manoeuver. Generally, choking to death is rare with puree diets, but it has occurred.
- Beware of cough medicines when your parent seems to have a cold. Your parent's cough is a lifesaving device, and cough medicines that suppress coughing also enhance the risk of aspiration. Not uncommonly a demented person's nocturnal cough is not a typical cough at all but rather repeated episodes of salivary aspiration.

Despite all of this effort, the time will come when the problem of aspiration of food and drink forces a critical decision. Typically the crisis shapes up as a pair of mutually exclusive fatalities—if given normal amounts of food and drink, the demented person will develop aspiration pneumonia; if food and drink are reduced in amount to reduce the risk of aspiration, weight loss, malnutrition, or dehydration will develop.

There is a technical solution to this predicament, and that is the use of tube feeding. Whether it is wise to grasp this "solution" is a moral and ethical question discussed in the next chapter. From a dispassionate technocratic perspective, however, the choice of tube feeding is generally either a nasogastric tube or a gastrostomy tube.

The nasogastric tube is inserted through the nose and into the stomach. A newer generation of tubes originally developed for children have been found to be more comfortable and should be the modern standard of care with persons of all ages. The tubes are not uncomfortable once they are inserted. Mentally healthy persons who have needed such tubes temporarily usually report that they are not painful, but demented persons cannot understand the meaning of the tube and invariably pull the tube out after a short time. This presents your parent with either the discomfort of repeated reinsertions of the tube or the discomfort of having restraints put on the hands to preserve the tube.

If tube feeding is to be done for more than a few days of temporary illness, the surgically implanted gastrostomy tube is much preferred. This tube is inserted directly through the skin into the stomach and overall is much more comfortable. Because it is tucked out of sight beneath the clothing, most demented persons do not indicate any physical or psychological annoyance by gastrostomy tubes. The necessity for light anesthesia and simple surgery to insert the tube should never be a reason to prefer the more uncomfortable nasal tube. The risk of fatal complication is very low (just tenths of a percent). Such small risk of death should never be allowed to justify discomfort or suffering for a person with dementia.

The Vegetative State: The term "vegetative state" designates a form of existence marked by a total inability to communicate with the outside world, and indeed a complete lack of any sign of awareness of the outside world. This state of existence is the result of the introduction of "halfway technology" into the disease process of dementia. Halfway technology is any technology that can extend the life expectancy of a sick person without being able to cure the person's underlying disease. In the natural world, the life of a demented person would not reach this state, death intervening earlier either by pneumonia or by malnutrition. Tube feeding, however, allows the body to be supported for months or years past the natural dying point. During this time of artificially extended life, dementia may continue to progress, creating a state of vegetative existence that is not to be found in nature.

As the child of a demented parent, you need to fully contemplate this vision of an uninhabited living body. This is a subject you should discuss with others in the family and if possible also with clergy. You need to plumb the depths of your religious and philosophical understanding of life; if possible, you need to reflect upon your parent's life and philosophy as well. Armed with your best moral guideposts, you will be as ready as possible to consider the issues posed in chapter 22.

22

The Right Time to Let Go

AS YOUR PARENT'S DEMENTIA reaches its final stages, the odds of coming into contact with hospital medicine increase tremendously, and indeed most demented persons will already have had at least one hospitalization. Most Americans die beneath the roof of a hospital, whether they have dementia or not. As your parent's dementia worsens, you need to examine the process of hospital medicine and decide when and how the system can benefit your mother or father.

With the exception of hospice programs, doctors, hospitals, and most modern health care institutions operate by the application of technological solutions to disease-related problems, for the purposes of extending life and avoiding death. It is a system that should genuinely strive to provide as much comfort as it does cure for sick people, and will do so if the two goals are compatible. When comfort and cure are incompatible, however, it is invariable that the drive to cure dominates the wish to console. In the pursuit of the maximum chance of cure, patients will lie inside magnetic coils and on hard metal tables; their hands will be tied to preserve the intravenous needle; pain medication will be withheld while the source of the pain is observed and examined.

The curative potential of scientific medicine depends a great deal on its quantitative approach to the patient. Repetitive blood tests may be an irritant to patients, but to the doctors the tests generate either constant reassurance or early warning of internal organ functions drifting abnormally high or low. Because so much of the power of modern medicine lies in the numbers it can measure and adjust, there is a temptation to fixate exclusively upon the numbers to the exclusion of the patient.

None of this is necessarily "bad medicine." It is, however, invasive, scientific, and technological medicine, and its justification is that the patient, once saved, will appreciate the cure and forgive the discomfort that attended it. If the benefit of cure is also your goal on behalf of your mom or dad, then your parent will be well served by the health care system. You will be in complete harmony with the system; its wheels are turning in the direction in which you wish to go.

Conflict between hospital doctors and family members develops when their goals diverge. At some point in the dementia process, many families find that the "benefits of cure" can no longer be appreciated. Sons and daughters may question the value of uncomfortable tests and treatments when the days being purchased cannot be appreciated by their mother or father; when the only "benefit" that mom or dad may live to experience is a still greater number of days full of ceaseless discomfort.

Realize that you too may, at some point, wish to stop the wheels of the health care machine in order to allow your parent an earlier, unimpeded exit from this world. If you can anticipate such a scenario, you will need to be prepared. Do not imagine that the momentum of the health care machinery will halt simply because you shout "Halt." How do you prepare yourself to be in a position to take control of the system at the point where you deem it necessary? Again, there are several steps to take (and all should be done earlier rather than later):

- *Guardianship.* For all of the reasons described earlier, you should seek to be named your parent's guardian if at all possible. It will enhance your legal status in making quality of life decisions and refusing life-sustaining treatment. If you are completely frustrated by the hospital system, guardianship will allow you to sign your parent out of the institution.

- *Living Will and Health Care Proxy.* Investigate living wills and health care proxies. Do not assume that your parent's living will, if one was made, will be recognized as a legal document. In some states, a living will, replete with legal language and notary stamps, is viewed as a nonbinding expression of the person's opinion at the time and nothing more. The living will may need to be augmented by the naming of a health care proxy—a person (presumably you) named by your parent *while mentally competent,* generally with witnessed signatures. If your state requires a health care proxy in order to enforce the wishes of the living will, you need to get this paperwork done *as early as possible after the diagnosis of dementia has been made.* Your parent's signature on the form needs to be affixed and dated at a time when an arguable claim to mental capacity can be made, lest your designation as the health care proxy be suspect or rejected

- *DNR.* Enquire about the rules for DNR in your state. The designation "DNR" stands for "do not resuscitate," which means that if your parent should experience an arrest of breathing or of cardiac function, no effort would be made to institute CPR (cardiopulmonary resuscitation). CPR not only involves manual compression of the chest, electrical shocks, and stimulant medication, but also involves connecting your parent to a respirator as part of the process.

Very serious consideration ought to be given to making every person with moderate dementia "DNR" on the basis of several compassionate arguments:

1. The prospects for success from the CPR procedure are not high. The brains of elderly persons afflicted with dementia are much more susceptible to damage from any time delay in starting CPR. Many readers may be aware of

the four-minute rule in trying to revive a person whose heart has stopped, the rule being that the average person's brain will undergo irreversible brain damage if the heart is not restarted within four minutes after it has stopped. This rule does not apply to elderly persons with dementia, and in them further brain damage will begin in much less than four minutes, making it even more improbable that the cardiac arrest team will be able to achieve a technically optimal CPR with no new neurological damage suffered during the process.

2. The process of CPR is uncomfortable, and so too is the intensive care unit, which is where the survivors of a CPR attempt are invariably taken. There in the intensive care unit, connected to a mechanical breathing device or respirator, patients lie unable to speak with the respirator tube in place. If the patient is agitated or struggling to remove the tube, their hands will be tied down; this is the case too if their stuggle threatens to dislodge any of the other tubes attached to intravenous solutions, drainage bags, or monitors. Each monitor adds its own noisy beeps to the cacophony of beeps being made by the monitors for other patients. For your mom or dad, tied down and unable to speak, there is no sense of day or night, no sense of what is happening. No one can tell if they are in pain; no one can tell if they are cold from air conditioning that is set for the comfort of the staff. Indeed, the intensive care unit can be so stressful even to healthy people that they have been reported to cause a type of nervous breakdown called ICU psychosis.

3. Remember that dementia is a process of progressive deterioration. Survival today offers only the promise of worse suffering and disability tomorrow. If the opportunity for a good death—sudden and painless—suddenly presents itself to a victim of advanced dementia, it may not be the wisest choice to chase it away using all the technological powers of modern medicine. Most people contemplating a choice of deaths would prefer for them-

selves a mercifully brief illness rather than months or years of suffering. By designating your mom or dad as DNR, you ensure that the opportunity for a quick and easy death, if it should appear, will not be refused. It is an opportunity that may not come again, and it may well be your mom or dad who suffers for its loss.

4. DNR designation does not change any aspect of medical care except the behavior of the staff at your parent's bedside in the event of sudden death. Antibiotics, oxygen, surgery, hospitalization—whatever else your parent may need is not discouraged by your parent's being DNR. Families sometimes refuse DNR designation from a mildly paranoid suspicion that it will be used as a shorthand signal to deny the demented person first-class medical care.

Once you have had your parent designated as DNR, there is no more you need to do about the contingency of sudden death. When and if your parent has a heart attack, the DNR designation will hopefully ensure that passage from life is quiet, peaceful, and accepted with a gracious dignity.

The weight of responsibility of guardianship or of health care proxy do not end when the paper is signed. You are now responsible for giving your approval or denial to medical treatment that would otherwise have proceeded on automatic pilot. How should you know what to approve and what to refuse?

The wisest rule you can follow is to choose a doctor that you trust—not only in terms of technical expertise but also in terms of human feeling and sensitivity. If you are fortunate in this regard, your guardianship or proxy responsibilities may be very much easier. Your power to refuse treatment may liberate your doctor from feeling a reluctant obligation to continue treatment according to the usual and customary medical standards. If your doctor shares your philosophical concerns and your confidence, it might be best not to attempt too fine a level of micromanagement of medical decisions.

If you must be more active, consider the following rules of compassionate care as decisions need to be made:

Rule 1: Never pass up a comfortable death to save your parent for an uncomfortable one in the future.

It is not your choice whether human life will or will not come to an end one day, but it may be your choice as to how it happens. There are some very uncomfortable ways of dying, including

- intestinal obstruction
- cancer of the bones
- suffocation by a buildup of fluid in the lung
- internal hemorrhage

By comparison, some forms of death are not unpleasant, at least as reported by those who have nearly died from them. Included in this group are

- dehydration
- infection
- starvation

If your parent's life has been made into one of constant suffering by dementia, you are under no moral obligation to prevent the occurrence of a natural and comfortable death. There is no law that requires everyone with a fever to receive antibiotics.

Rule 2: Do not allow your mom or dad to live longer than God would have allowed.

To this end, one must stipulate instructions for "no tube feeding" and "no artificial hydration." Some states will not allow such a stipulation by a health care proxy unless it was made in writing at the time your parent designated you as proxy. For this reason, it is key that the legal details be understood and complied with *years before* the situation is likely to develop.

The issue of tube feeding is the true Rubicon of dementia. The general public and lawyers continue to draw up documents that anticipate being "comatose" or "terminally ill" or "having no hope of survival," but these are all based upon a television soap-opera understanding of the end of life. A typical end-stage demented person lying contracted in bed, being fed by a gastrostomy tube, able only to scream in pain when his decubitus ulcers are dressed—*that person would meet none of the usual "living will" criteria!*

In medical terminology, "comatose" is defined as being unresponsive to pain, and such a patient is not "in a coma" even if profoundly vegetative! Likewise, "terminally ill" in medical parlance means being within a few months of certain—yet with the benefit of tube feeding, such a person may not be certain of death for a year or more. And how is "no hope of survival" to be interpreted? The problem for such a demented person is precisely that survival in pain has been artificially created by the technology of tube feeding.

Under a set of guidelines precluding the use of tube or intravenous sustenance, your parent would continue to live as long as the will to eat and drink remain alive. As these desires or abilities fade, your parent would easily slip into death in a few days or weeks. Additionally, by refusing tube feeding or intravenous fluid, you potentially allow your father or mother one final expression of power over their own bodies—the ability to remove themselves from a world too painful to endure by the simple act of closing their mouth.

Rule 3: If your parent has a painful condition, assume they have pain. Never stint on pain medication for fear of anything, including the fear that its use may hasten death.

Narcotic pain medications are sometimes underused in frail persons because the drugs can depress the respiratory centers of the brain, leading to death (a very comfortable one, in fact). Respiratory depression is an eventuality more feared than realized, yet it is the fear that drives many doctors' decision making. The result is epidemic underprescribing of pain medication.

If your parent has a painful condition, assume that they suffer pain, and ensure that a physician prescribes a dose of pain medication that is adequate for an average person with the same condition. Insofar as your parent will not be able to ask for the medication, see that it is given "around the clock" on the assumption that they might be having pain at any time. Choices include the following:

- Tylenol, by mouth or suppository, every four hours, for mild sources of pain like arthritis
- Tylenol with codeine, by mouth only, every four to six hours for more serious pain like fractures or moderate decubitus ulcers
- Morphine, by mouth or by skin patch, for deep decubitus ulcers extending to the bone or for cancer. Morphine patches are especially useful, available in a variety of strengths and each one able to administer continuous morphine absorbed through the skin.

Rule 4:   Hospice is not just for cancer patients.

The only place in the health care system where comfort is clearly stressed over cure is in a hospice program. The familiarity of the general public with hospice programs generally comes from awareness of their work with younger persons dying of cancer, but hospice service is open to any person afflicted with a terminal disease. A person with severe dementia who is not able to eat and drink to maintain weight, and who is not to be placed on tube feeding, is truly a "terminal patient." Indeed, by measuring the rate of weight loss each week, assuming death on or before reaching seventy pounds, one may project the life expectancy of a demented person more precisely than that of many cancer patients. Hospice programs offer a wealth of assistance and support for both you and your parent.

Rule 5: If your parent is dying at home, never call "911."

Ambulance crews do not rush to the scene to lend assistance; they come to take people to the hospital. In a world populated by people of variable sanity, most 911 ambulance crews operate under a set of policy guidelines that do not allow anyone—family, private doctor, or a demented person—to "interfere" with their official responsibilities. If you call 911 to help lift your parent from the floor, not only may you be unable to stop the crew from taking your parent to the hospital, but they may go to a hospital not of your choosing.

If you call 911 because your parent is having difficulty in breathing, you may be powerless to stop the crew from initiating CPR—indeed, some ambulance crews will initiate CPR routinely, even if the call was placed for a person who was intended to die at home. Ambulance crews are not lawyers. They do not know if you are in fact the person's relative or are not; they have neither the time nor the inclination to examine your guardianship papers or your health care proxy to see if it is valid; they do not know if the person named in the document is truly you. When you call 911, expect that you may not establish authority again until the dust settles in the hospital.

If you wish to have your parent die at home, therefore, do not call 911 for anything! If your parent has already died, call your doctor; if he or she not available, call the funeral home. They can call the police precinct and calmly report that your parent has been terminally ill for some time and passed away at home. Details for the pronouncement of death and a death certificate can then be worked out.

Rule 6:   There's no place like home.

Until death occurs, the only way to remain in absolute control of the process is to keep your parent at home. If your parent is already living in a nursing home, then the nursing home *is their home*. When the time has come to no longer resist the approach of death, you should forcefully use your guardianship or proxy authority to state that henceforth your parent is not to be hospitalized for any reason without your explicit consent. Specify what kinds of treatment you consider acceptable or unacceptable—antibiotics, pain medication, oxygen, etc.—to the degree that you have formed strong opinions for or against any of these.

Many nursing homes tend to ship their residents to a hospital at the first sign of illness, professing that the level of care that a nursing home can provide cannot hope to provide the same potential for cure as that of a hospital. This is true but irrelevant. In the first place, in the advanced state of dementia, the benefits of cure should always be subordinated to the benefits of comfort, which the nursing home will optimize. In the second place, even though "nursing home medicine" is inferior to hospital medicine, the typical American nursing home has medical resources that outshine many hospitals in the less developed countries of this world. Do not be surprised if you have reconciled yourself to your parent's comfortable death in the nursing home only to see mom or dad recover!

If your parent is still at home, your capacity to create a comfortable and loving environment is optimized, but so too is the mental stress upon you. Remember that death at home has become somewhat strange and frightening, but not because dying has changed, only because dying at home went out of fashion over the past few decades. For the previous centuries, all families had as regular experience with preparing for death as they did with preparing for birth. In order for you to recapture this lost skill, you will need only two things: courage and supplies.

Courage will be needed when you discover that time spent with a dying mother or father seems very long indeed, although in retrospect it will always be remembered as special and mystical time. In real life, it takes much longer to die than is portrayed on TV and in films. Dehydration may take a week or more. A "fatal" pneumonia sometimes get better, as it was known to do in the pre-antibiotic era. The predictable death of a person who has stopped eating and drinking may be less predictable if suddenly eating and drinking resume. Most of the emotional strain reported by families who experience the death of a loved one at home comes not from the final agonal moments of death but rather the length of time spent dying.

What do you need to ensure a comfortable death for your parent at home? The following is a list of what you will need and why it will be useful:

- *Oxygen*. It is possible that your parent will benefit from having oxygen available during the final days at home, but it is a certainty that *you* will benefit from having it available.

  Witnessing the final hours of a dying person is especially difficult for families to bear, in part because a dying person displays various unusual patterns of deep rapid respirations, irregular gasps, and temporary halts in breathing. Most of these breathing pattern abnormalities are due to the dying process itself, during which the brain's "breathing center" becomes disorganized and starts to fumble the process of breathing. There is no discomfort, since by this time the brain has been thoroughly numbed into unconsciousness.

  Families, however, tend to be frightened by what they see. They watch this irregular pattern of gasps and deep rapid respirations and assume that mom or dad must be having trouble breathing. Having oxygen available will allow you to reassure yourself that you are doing at home as much as anyone in the hospital would be doing at that moment.

- *Morphine patches*. These patches allow you to exert hospital-level control over two of death's most unwelcome fellow travelers—pain and difficulty breathing. If your mom or dad appears to be in pain, or if dying is accompanied by a disease likely to bring true difficulty in breathing—pneumonia, heart failure, or fluid in the lungs—these patches can be the equivalent of injections of morphine on a regular basis. Doctors use morphine not only for pain but also to ease the breathing difficulty of patients when oxygen alone does not suffice. Each patch lasts for three days and comes in a variety of strengths. With these patches available, you need not wonder whether something more could have been done in hospital for your parent's comfort.
- *Tylenol suppositories*. Useful for mild pain, but also for fever if you feel that fever is making your parent uncomfortable. This is not always the case, unless the fever is very high. It is always the case, however, that fever will hasten dehydration and hasten death. If you are a bit frightened and not yet ready, rectal suppositories of Tylenol may help relieve your anxieties and assure you that again you are doing the same procedure as would be performed in the hospital.
- *Compazine suppositories*. Compazine is one of the most effective medications for controlling vomiting. Although vomiting is not a part of the dying process, it may be part of the disease from which your parent is dying. Available in pill form, compazine is actually less valuable in this form, since patients who are nauseated tend to regurgitate the very medicine meant to help. In the hospital, therefore, compazine or similar medications are given by injection. Without the skill to inject medications, you can control vomiting by giving the suppository by rectum every eight to twelve hours.

These few items comprise the tools you may need to successfully and comfortably midwife your parent from this world into the next. If certain features of your parent's condition require more, your doctor or the hospice will be able to tell you.

In addition to these comfort measures, your doctor may, by ingrained reflex, offer to prescribe an additional spectrum of home medical technology to treat your parent and defer the moment of death. This may include a wide variety of services being provided by private home care agencies, including home blood tests, X rays, intravenous fluids, and potent antibiotics administered intravenously by registered nurses.

One important caution about such home medical treatment is called for:

Remember what you are trying to accomplish!

If you feel that death is the welcome and natural end to your parent's suffering, it makes no sense to take a combative stance to resist death with intravenous fluid and antibiotics. It may lead to your parent's unanticipated survival and continued pain. If despite such home medical treatment your parent dies anyway, such treatment will almost certainly have prolonged the dying process pointlessly and possibly uncomfortably.

There is no ethically right or wrong choice for every individual. You will need to make your decision based upon your moral and religious training. There is such a thing, however, as moral cowardice. Before you make any decision on behalf of your mother or father, you must submit yourself to a pair of moral tests:

- **Test 1:** You must be certain that what you do will be done only for your parent's welfare, not yours. Your parent must not be obliged to continue living in pain because you, the child, are not yet prepared to say goodbye to Mom or Dad.
- **Test 2:** You must be honest with yourself about which choice you are making. You must not secretly wish for

death to release your parent from the suffering of advanced dementia yet kowtow to real or imagined pressure to permit curative treatment to continue.

Beyond these moral guideposts, nothing is certain but your heart. May God be with you.

Afterword

As you reflect upon the years spent in caring for a demented parent, from diagnosis to death, you will be struck by the number of transformations that have occurred.

You will have witnessed the transformation of your parent from the reliable bulwark of your youth to a helpless creature dependent upon the mercy of others.

Regardless of your age when the disease first appeared, by now you will see in retrospect the transformation that has taken place in you, molding you from the grown child you were then into the fully mature adult you are now, seasoned by one of life's toughest experiences.

You will have noted how even the process of dementia changed while you watched—what was initially an experience of essentially mental suffering became a state of physical discomfort by the end.

But mostly you will have witnessed a struggle for power. Dealing with dementia is largely a struggle to concentrate in your hands the power and authority required to preserve the comfort and safety of your parent. Initially the struggle rests between the parent and the child; by the late stages of dementia, the struggle is between the child and the health care system. If you have been successful at optimizing your parent's independence, mental peace, and physical comfort, it has likely been due to your willingness to be a strenuous advocate on your parent's behalf in a world that would regard your parent as a problem.

By engaging yourself actively in the care of your demented parent, you have returned the gift of self-sacrificing love that was once given to you. And you will have learned from your parent one of life's last and most important lessons—that it is not death that is the enemy of human life. The enemy is suffering.

As the wheel of life turns in your direction, it may be worthwhile to reflect upon this lesson. It may be the last important thing that your mom or dad was able to teach you.

Glossary

Alzheimer's Disease. One of the diseases that can cause dementia. Some consider it the major cause of dementia in the elderly today, although small-stroke disease also has a claim to this title. The mechanism by which Alzheimer's disease causes brain damage and dementia is not known exactly, although under the microscope the brains of patients with Alzheimer's disease show deposits of abnormal protein as well as areas of dying, tangled brain cells.

Anti-cholinergic. A term applied to drugs that interfere with the chemical choline. The human body uses choline in a variety of ways in different organs. Anticholinergic drugs generally have certain side effects in common, including dry mouth, constipation, possible aggravation of glaucoma, and impairment of short-term memory.

Antidepressant Drug. Any drug which can alleviate depression by changing the balance of brain chemicals, called neurotransmitters, which are now felt to be a major factor of most cases of depression. There are a variety of these neurotransmitters, as well as a variety of antidepressant drugs which raise or lower their concentrations in the brain. All are prescription drugs.

Benign Forgetfulness. The common type of forgetfulness that appears at about age 30 and gradually worsens with age. In benign forgetfulness, remembered information is not lost, but its retrieval when needed can be delayed long enough to cause impatience and frustration. This condition is *not* associated with dementia.

CAT Scan. An image made by an X ray machine that uses computers rather than photographic film to display its pictures, the result being a lifelike cross-section of the part of the body being scanned. Used to obtain cross-sectional pictures of the brain in patients being evaluated for dementia.

Catastrophic Reaction. An uncontrollable tantrum of screaming, agitation, or paranoid fear, occurring in a demented patient who has become overwhelmed by stress or stimulation.

CPR. The abbreviation for "cardiopulmonary resuscitation," the process of restarting the heart and lungs in a person technically dead. CPR generally involves pressure on the breastbone to maintain the circulation of the body, along with administration of stimulant medications and electrical shocks to restart the heart. Generally the process involves the passage of a breathing tube down the throat and into the patient's airway, permitting the patient to be connected to an automatic respirator or breathing machine.

Delusion. The misinterpretation of one object as another, such as believing a coat lying on the couch is a person.

Dementia. A general term implying the progressive destruction of brain tissue over time, with the production of worsening degrees of intellectual deterioration. The term does not specify any one disease, and many disease processes (Alzheimer's disease, small-stroke disease, syphilis, AIDS, and several others) can cause dementia.

DNR. The abbreviation for "do not resuscitate," the decision made either by family or patient that in the event of death an attempt will not be made to restart the heart by cardiopulmonary resuscitation (*see* CPR).

False Negative. A type of error in a diagnostic test, in which the test result suggests that the patient is normal, when in fact the patient is not well and it is the test that is incorrect.

False Positive. A type of error in a diagnostic test, in which the test results suggests that something is wrong with the patient, when in fact the patient is normal and the test is wrong.

Gastro-Colic Reflex. One of the earliest reflexes, present at birth, reflex expulsion of bowel contents when the stomach is expanded by a feeding.

Hallucination. An imaginary figment created by the brain. Unlike a delusion, there does not need to be any object to be misidentified—the entire vision is created in the mind.

Incontinence.   The inability to retain voluntary control over the elimination of urine or feces.

Long-Term Memory.   Memory of events that occurred months or usually years ago. These memories are stored in the brain in a manner unknown at the present time but clearly different from the way that short-term memories are stored. Part of the difference is the greater resistance of long term-memory to the destructive effects of dementia.

Malignant Forgetfulness.   A pattern of forgetfulness in which there is a failure in memory recall because the memory being sought has been obliterated from the brain; this pattern is not part of normal aging, and is suggestive of brain damage by dementia.

Meningioma.   A tumor or swelling of the tissue called the meninges, which covers the surface of the brain. Although these tumors are benign in the sense that they do not spread to other parts of the body like malignant cancers, they can cause local brain damage if large enough to exert damaging pressure on the surface of the brain.

Meningitis.   An infection of the tissue covering the surface of the brain (the meninges). Most of these cases are obvious and serious infections and treated as such, but some low-grade, chronic cases of meningitis may not look very much like infections but may imitate the slow destruction of brain tissue that is typical of dementia.

MRI Scan.   A computerized scan of the body, looking very much like a CAT scan in providing a detailed cross-sectional picture of the part of the body being studied. Unlike the CAT scan, the MRI scan uses magnetic fields rather than X rays to generate its pictures. MRI scans are slightly superior to CAT scans in their ability to show the damage of small-stroke dementia.

Multi-Infarct Disease.   Another name for small-stroke disease. One of the two major causes of dementia, along with Alzheimer's disease. The progressive damage to the brain is caused by the accumulation of injury caused by small strokes.

Nocturnal Awakening.   A type of insomnia in which there is no problem falling asleep initially, but afterward sleep does not continue through the night.

Organic Brain Syndrome (OBS).   An outdated term for dementia, it is still found in some books and articles.

Paradoxical Diarrhea. Cases of severe constipation in which the constipated stool is too hard and too large to be eliminated. Instead, the stool remains in the colon as an irritant, causing watery diarrhea as the colon tries unsuccessfully to expel it.

Parkinson's Disease. A disease marked by stiff muscle movement, involuntary shaking of the hand, and stooped posture. Approximately 25 percent of cases are associated with dementia.

Pseudodementia. Severe forgetfulness and dysfunctional behavior that bear a close superficial resemblance to dementia but are actually due to severe depression.

Retrograde Amnesia. A specific pattern of memory loss over time, starting with the destruction of a person's most recent memories, progressing to the destruction of older and older memories as the damage from dementia advances.

Senility. An outdated term for dementia, implying incorrectly that dementia comes from aging alone. It is now understood that normal aging is not accompanied by the changes which we call dementia. Dementia is the result of a specific number of diseases.

Short-Term Memory. Memory for recent events, generally covering a time span from minutes to weeks. Short-term memory is held by the brain in a manner unknown at the present time but especially vulnerable to the damage caused by dementia.

Sleep Induction. The process of falling asleep.

Small-Stroke Disease. One of the two major diseases causing dementia, the other being Alzheimer's disease. The damage to the brain in this illness is caused by the accumulation of multiple areas of brain injury due to the occurrence of multiple small or silent strokes.

Smiling Depression. A type of depression in which the sufferer is particularly adept at acting cheerful and disguising the degree to which depression exists.

Spinal Tap. A diagnostic test in which a thin needle is passed into the spinal canal from a point generally in the small of the back. At this site, samples of the fluid that bathe the brain can be extracted for study.

Subdural Hematoma (SDH). A blood clot located beneath the protective blanket of surrounding tissue called the dura. If large enough, such a blood clot can cause brain damage by the pressure injury it exerts on the underlying brain surface.

Sundowning. A pattern of confusion, disorientation, and hallucination that may be one of the earliest signs of dementia. It typically occurs in an individual who during the day may seem nearly normal but who begins to show the above signs of disordered thinking in the late afternoon or early evening, when the sun goes down.

Drug Reference List

Ambien.   A sedative that constitutes its own class of medication (imidazopyridine), its generic name is zolpidem tartrate. Reported to be less likely to cause a fall than many other sedatives, although absolute confidence should not be placed in this claim.

Ativan.   A tranquilizer of the benzodiazepine class. Its generic name is lorazepam, and it is a member of one of the most popular families of sedatives, the benzodiazepines. Its duration of action is approximately eight to twelve hours, making it a reasonable drug to use for daytime sedation or at night for sleep. As with all sedatives, risks include falling, excessive lethargy, and increased confusion, but among the benzodiazepines it is one of my preferences when used in low doses.

BuSpar.   The generic name for this is buspirone. BuSpar is a drug in a class of its own, being a tranquilizer with little or no sedative property. In theory it ought to be ideal, and on occasion it is, although I find it to be weak as well as gentle. It seems to work best to calm anxiety that manifests itself as a need for constant reassurance. It sometimes needs to be given for three or four weeks before reaching its full benefit, which can be a long time to wait for anxiety to come under control.

Chloral Hydrate.   A fast-acting sedative that has several credits—it is generally safe and usually eliminated by the body by morning. It is available as a liquid or suppository, making it valuable for patients who cannot swallow pills. The primary caution is not to mix it with alcohol, although this is true of every sedative. Overall a good choice when the sleeping difficulty is with falling asleep initially.

Cognex. The first of what promises to be a series of medications seeking to help increase memory for patients with Alzheimer's disease. There is no claim that it will help persons afflicted with other types of dementia, most importantly small-stroke dementia, and no claim that among Alzheimer's patients it can do more than modestly alleviate the symptoms of memory loss for a few hours. Its generic name is tacrine.

Unfortunately, it is a complicated medication with which to deal. Ironically for a "memory" medication, it needs to be given four times a day, a taxing task for many patients to perform. Additionally, a significant percentage of patients develop abnormal liver tests on the medication, although this does not necessarily mean the drug needs to be discontinued in all cases. Even when it works, the benefit is modest. Given the lack of anything better at the moment, most families have been pleased to continue the medication even for its modest benefit.

Dalmane. A very long acting sedative in the benzodiazepine family (Valium, Ativan, etc.). In my judgment, it is too long acting to warrant use in even the healthy elderly, no less those with dementia. Many doctors disagree and consider it a "safe" sleeping pill, but to my mind a safe sleeping pill should be out of the body by morning. Estimates of the elimination time for Dalmane have ranged up to one hundred hours. Its chemical name is flurazepam.

Desyrel. A sedating antidepressant with the generic name trazodone. It is a good choice when dealing with depression and sleeping problems at night, especially since it is relatively free of many of the other side effects of antidepressant drugs (particularly constipation and dizziness).

Dexedrine. A drug in the amphetamine class, it is more tightly controlled by the Drug Enforcement Administration (DEA) than the other drugs mentioned here. Used more in Europe than in the United States due to its street reputation, nevertheless it happens to be a fairly good drug for depressed demented patients. The issue of addiction is not a reason to rule out its use if it can lift the spirits of a dementia victim and often serve to stimulate appetite. The major caution in my mind is not the moral issue of addiction but the risk of heart attack if given to a patient with a serious cardiac condition. Overall it tends to be underused, which is unfortunate.

Ditropan. An anticholinergic drug with the chemical name oxybutynin, it is designed to relax the bladder (choline causing the bladder to contract). It does this well but cannot completely avoid the other anticholinergic side effects of dry mouth, constipation, and possibly increased confusion. These other effects tend to show up when the drug is used in higher doses during the day and night. If it is used in low doses and judiciously (just at night, perhaps, or just before traveling), I find that most people manage to avoid the side effects while obtaining about eight hours of relief from uncontrolled urine incontinence.

Doxepin. Doxepin is an antidepressant drug that is one of my favorites. Curiously for a favorite drug, it has several side effects—it is sedating and mildly anticholinergic. The combination plays very well, however, for a demented individual who is depressed and sleeping poorly due to the need to void several times at night. Doxepin not only helps to improve mood but also aids sleep both by being a sedative as well as by relaxing the bladder overnight. Add to this that it tends to stimulate appetite, and it is often the one drug that can target many of the common problems of the person with moderate dementia. Its least useful side effect is constipation, which is so predictable as to warrant the routine initiation of anti-constipation measures as soon as the drug is prescribed, rather than waiting for trouble to begin.

Halcion. The shortest-acting sedative in the benzodiazepine class (Ativan, Valium, etc.), its generic name is triazolam. For that reason, it ought to be the best in theory, but in practice it has been associated with serious problems from confusion or hallucination. I no longer use it except in rare individual circumstances, which are becoming even rarer.

Haldol. One of the most famous (or infamous) of all antipsychotic medications, its generic name is haloperidol. Some geriatric doctors pride themselves on never using these drugs, but I generally find such ideological opposition to be ill considered.

Its intended target is severely disorganized thinking accompanied by hallucination or agitation. Unlike tranquilizers such as Ativan or Valium, which are broadly used in the general population as well for sleep or anxiety, drugs like

Haldol are used only in dementia or for the treatment of psychosis or schizophrenia in younger populations. The side effects of Haldol account for its reputation. In high doses, it can cause patients to become stiff, rigid, unemotional, quiet, and depersonalized, as well as sometimes causing involuntary twitches of the face and mouth. I too find high doses of Haldol uncomfortable to use. In very low doses, however, the drug can sometimes work wonders by eliminating paranoid fears and hallucinations with little or no side effect. In low doses, it can be a valuable medication, particularly since it is also available as a tasteless liquid that mixes well with coffee and juice, as well as in the form of a long-acting, once-a-month injection. Either form may be a godsend for an agitated, paranoid individual for whom every pill to be swallowed is a battle to be fought.

Librium.   A tranquilizer drug of the benzodiazepine class with the chemical name chlordiazepoxide, Librium is typical of this class of drugs. It can be effective for control of anxiety and as a sleep aid, but it carries an appreciable risk of falling when used in an ambulatory patient, and a risk of either excessive sedation or increased confusion when used in any demented person.

Lomotil.   This drug is a combination of two chemicals, diphenoxylate and atropine. It is a typically anticholinergic drug, with the intended effect being to control diarrhea by slowing down the bowels. Like all anticholinergic drugs, it can never be given without some concern about dry mouth or increased confusion. More importantly, it should never be given unless it is certain that the diarrhea is not the paradoxical diarrhea of severe constipation.

Mellaril.   Its chemical name is thioridazine. Like Haldol, it is a type of tranquilizer never used in the general population, but confined to the most serious agitated psychoses of patients with either dementia or schizophrenia. It is much more sedating than Haldol and tends to be my choice if sleeping is an associated problem with paranoia, hallucination, agitation, etc., and I wish to try to hit two sets of symptoms with one medication. Concerns among higher doses include the same concerns as for Haldol—sedation, depersonalization, muscle stiffness, and involuntary movements.

Morphine Patches.   Available under several names, including Fentanyl Transdermal System and Duragesic, these patches release measured amounts of morphine into the body through the skin, offering twenty-four-hour pain relief without the need for injections or swallowing pills. In my experience, they are one of the great boons to the terminally ill, often allowing them to stay at home and die comfortably.

Persantine.   This drug, with the generic name dipyrimidole, is somewhat effective in inhibiting blood clots in the small circulation of the brain. It works best when combined with low doses of aspirin. Together they are far from a cure for small-stroke disease, but given the lack of anything superior, I tend to use the combination when determined to make a strong attempt to retard the progression of a dementia I believe to be caused by small strokes.

Prosom.   Another of the benzodiazepine class of tranquilizer-sedatives, this one with the chemical name estazolam. Use of this drug warrants the same cautions as all the rest—there is increased risk of falling, sedation, and increased confusion.

Prozac.   Chemical name fluoxetine. Prozac belongs to a new class of antidepressants called serotonin uptake inhibitors, named for the neurotransmitter serotonin, which is affected by the drugs in this group. Along with others in this group, including Paxil (paroxetine) and Zoloft (sertraline), Prozac is becoming one of the first-choice antidepressants in the elderly. The advantage of this group of antidepressants is that they have a relatively low level of side effects. If no other issue is to be addressed other than the treatment of depression, it appears reasonable to use either Prozac or one of its cousins as a first-choice treatment.

Restoril.   Another of the benzodiazepine-class tranquilizers, mentioned primarily to express my general avoidance. It has a long duration of action which leaves me concerned for daytime falling and sedation. Chemical name is temazepam.

Ritalin.   Its chemical name is methylphenidate. Like Dexedrine, it is drug in the amphetamine class and is tightly controlled by the DEA. It too is used more frequently in Europe than in the United States. Like Dexedrine, it also happens to be a fairly good drug for depressed demented patients. The major caution is not the moral issue of addiction but the risk of heart attack if given to a patient with a serious cardiac condition. Overall it too tends to be underused.

Xanax. Another member of the populous family of ben- zodiazepine tranquilizer-sedatives. Xanax (alprazolam) is a bit more useful than the others as a daytime drug, lasting about four hours. It is a good choice when only temporary calming is needed—for example, with a patient who is gener- ally relaxed during the day but who puts up a fight during bathtime. It is too short acting for sleep, however, and for that purpose I tend to favor Ativan.

Note: At the present time, there are over fifty drugs for Alzheimer's disease at some stage of development. Some of these are close to being released onto the market; some are far enough along the FDA approval process to be taking volunteers for drug-testing trials.

If you are interested in having your parent participate in an experimental drug trial, you can obtain up-to-date infor- mation by contacting the Alzheimer's Association at (312) 335-5792.

Appendix:
Alzheimer's Disease Centers

Baylor College of Medicine
Houston, Texas
Alzheimer's Disease Research Center
Department of Neurology
Baylor College of Medicine
6501 Fannin, NB302
Houston, TX 77030-3498
713-798-4073

Case Western Reserve University
Cleveland, Ohio
Alzheimer's Disease Research Center
University Hospitals of Cleveland
11100 Euclid Avenue
Cleveland, OH 44106
216-844-7360

Columbia University
New York, New York
Alzheimer's Disease Research Center
Columbia University Department of Pathology
630 West 168th Street
New York, NY 10032
212-305-3300

Duke University Medical Center
Durham, North Carolina
Principal Investigator and Director
Joseph and Kathleen Bryan Alzheimer's Disease Research
2200 W. Main Street, Suite A-230
Durham, NC 27705
919-286-3228

Emory University
Decatur, Georgia 30033
Emory Alzheimer's Disease Center
VA Medical Center (151)
1670 Clairmont Road
Decatur, Georgia 30033
404-728-7714

Harvard Medical School
Boston, Massachusetts
Department of Neurology ACC 830
Massachusetts General Hospital
15 Parkman Street
Boston, MA 02114
617-726-1728

Indiana University
Indianapolis, Indiana
Department of Pathology
635 Barnhill Drive, MS-A142
Indianapolis, IN 46202-5120
317-274-7818

Johns Hopkins University School of Medicine
Baltimore, Maryland
The John Hopkins University School of Medicine
558 Ross Research Building
720 Rutland Avenue
Baltimore, MD 21205-2196
410-955-5632

Mayo Clinic
Rochester, Minnesota
Mayo Clinic
200 First Street, SW
Rochester, MN 55905
507-284-4006

Mount Sinai School of Medicine
New York, New York
Mount Sinai School of Medicine
One Gustave L. Levy Place, Box #1230
New York, NY 10029-6574
212-241-6623

New York University
New York, New York
New York University Medical Center
550 First Avenue, Room THN 312B
New York, NY 10016
212-263-5703

Oregon Health Sciences University
Portland, Oregon
Oregon Health Sciences University
3181 S.W. Sam Jackson Park Road
Portland, OR 97201
503-494-7321

Rush-Presbyterian-St. Lukes Medical Center
Chicago, Illinois
Rush-Presbyterian-St. Lukes Medical Center
Rush Institute on Aging
1645 West Jackson Boulevard, Suite 675
Chicago, IL 60612
312-942-3350

University of Alabama
Birmingham, Alabama
University of Alabama at Birmingham
1720 7th Avenue South Sparks Center 454
Birmingham, AL 35294-0017
205-934-3847

University of California, Davis
Berkeley, California
University of California, Davis
Northern California Alzheimer's Disease Center
Alta Bate Medical Center
2001 Dwight Way
Berkeley, CA 94704
510-204-4530

University of California, Los Angeles
Los Angeles, California
710 Westwood Plaza
Los Angeles, CA 90024-1769
310-206-5238

University of California, San Diego
San Diego, California
UCSD School of Medicine
9500 Gilman Drive (0624)
La Jolla, CA 92093-0624
619-534-4606

University of Kansas
Kansas City, Kansas
University of Kansas Medical Center
3901 Rainbow Blvd., Wescoe Pav. 1008
Kansas City, KS 66160-7314
913-588-6094

University of Kentucky
Lexington, Kentucky
Sanders-Brown Research Center on Aging
101 Sanders-Brown Building
University of Kentucky
Lexington, KY 40536-0230
606-323-6040

University of Michigan
Ann Arbor, Michigan
Michigan Alzheimer's Disease Research Center
University of Michigan
1914 Taubman Center
Ann Arbor, MI 48109-0316
313-936-9070

University of Pennsylvania
Philadelphia, Pennsylvania
University of Pennsylvania School of Medicine
Room A009, Basement Maloney/HUP
36th and Spruce Streets
Philadelphia, PA 19104-4283
215-662-6921 or 6399

University of Pittsburgh
Pittsburgh, Pennsylvania
Alzheimer's Disease Research Center
University of Pittsburgh
Western Psychiatric Institute and Clinic
3811 O'Hara Street
Pittsburgh, PA 15213
412-624-6889

University of Rochester
Rochester, New York
University of Rochester Medical Center
601 Elmwood Avenue
Rochester, NY 14642
716-275-2581

University of Southern California
Los Angeles, California
University of California, Irvine
University of Southern California
Andrus Gerontology Center
University Park, MC 0191
3715 McClintock Avenue
University of Southern California
Los Angeles, CA 90089-0191
213-740-1758

University of Texas Southwestern Medical Center
Dallas, Texas
University of Texas
Southwestern Medical Center
5323 Harry Hines Boulevard
Dallas, TX 75235-9036
214-648-3239

University of Washington
Seattle, Washington
University of Washington
Seattle, WA 98195
206-543-5088

Washington University Medical Center
Saint Louis, Missouri
Alzheimer's Disease Research Center
Campus Box 8111
Washington University School of Medicine
660 S. Euclid Avenue
Saint Louis, MO 63110
314-286-2881

Index

About the Author

DR. KENNETH P. SCILEPPI received his medical training in the New York City hospital system, beginning with medical school at SUNY Downstate in Brooklyn and completing his residency at the Bronx Municipal Hospital. He received his training in geriatric medicine in 1979 at Cornell University Medical Center and was selected as the first DeWitt Wallace Fellow in Geriatric Medicine. On staff at Cornell University Medical Center since 1979, he has published several research papers in osteoporosis, Alzheimer's disease, and health policy for the elderly. After serving as Medical Director for the Elderplan Social/Health Maintenance Organization, he established his present private practice in geriatric medicine in New York City.